The Flowers of Tarbes
or, Terror in Literature

The Flowers of Tarbes

or, Terror in Literature

JEAN PAULHAN

Translated and with
an Introduction by Michael Syrotinski

University of Illinois Press
Urbana and Chicago

Library of Congress Cataloging-in-Publication Data
Paulhan, Jean, 1884–1968.
[Fleurs de Tarbes, ou, La terreur dans les lettres. English]
The flowers of Tarbes, or, Terror in literature / Jean Paulhan ;
translated from the French and with an introduction
by Michael Syrotinski.
p.   cm.
Includes bibliographical references.
ISBN-13: 978-0-252-03019-2 (cloth : alk. paper)
ISBN-10: 0-252-03019-2 (cloth : alk. paper)
1. French literature—History and criticism.
2. Literature—Psychology.
I. Title: Flowers of Tarbes.
II. Title: Terror in literature.
III. Syrotinski, Michael, 1957–
IV. Title.
PQ145.P3813   2006
840.9'353—dc22   2005009416

Contents

Acknowledgments

I would like to thank Jacqueline Paulhan and the Société des Lecteurs de Jean Paulhan for their support, my colleagues Margaret Jubb and Alison Saunders for their generous assistance in translating some of the more perplexing details of the text, and Bernard Baillaud, who very generously shared his encyclopedic bibliographical knowledge in helping to illuminate the most elusive and obscure names in the glossary. Knowing that a handful of these references have eluded even him is a reliable indication that we are probably straying into the realm of the playfully apocryphal, to which Jean Paulhan was certainly not averse. I am extremely grateful to Willis Regier for inviting me to publish *The Flowers of Tarbes* with the University of Illinois Press, and immensely appreciative of the enthusiastic endorsement of the translation by its two readers, Ann Smock and Jordan Stump, whose editorial suggestions were also most helpful. My greatest debt, though, as ever, is to Christine Laennec for her unerring instinct, her perpetually wise insights, and her invaluable assistance and encouragement in the final stages of the project.

Translator's Introduction

Although he is largely unknown to an anglophone readership, Jean Paulhan was a central figure in the literary landscape of twentieth-century France, both as an influential editor and as an often polemical essayist. Paulhan himself considered *The Flowers of Tarbes or, Terror in Literature* to be his most important work, and a distillation of his thinking about language and literature. Like many of Paulhan's related texts on the theory and practice of literature, *The Flowers of Tarbes* has a deceptive naïveté and period charm about it, and ostensibly owes more to nineteenth- and early twentieth-century writers and critics who had long been unfashionable, even by the time Paulhan was writing, than to what we usually take as the major points of reference of linguistic and literary theory in the twentieth century. To read *The Flowers of Tarbes* is to be drawn into this other rather arcane and archaic world. It was written at a time when literary critics were still highly respected professionals with a visible public profile, and even though the predictable and well-ordered literary world was a far cry from the cut and thrust of our contemporary theoretical arena, there was no less intensity and urgency in the stakes being contested. Paulhan was certainly not afraid of engaging in head-to-head polemics, and in many ways this text could be seen to define a critical moment in the history of criticism. In taking on the "establishment," as it were (the great figures of his own and the previous generation, such as Rémy de Gourmont, Antoine Albalat, Marcel Schwob, Pierre Lasserre, and so on), Paulhan was already performing a subtle, but radical, destabilization of the activity of reading (and writing) literature. My intention and hope in appending a glossary of basic information on writers, critics, and other less familiar names either directly quoted or alluded to by Paulhan in his narrative is to bring to life the half-forgotten, now rather neglected world of his time. It seemed useful to contextualize *The Flowers of Tarbes* in this way in order to create a sense of this cultural milieu, and to underline the sheer diversity of references that would probably have been more or less immediately recognizable to Paulhan and his contemporaries.

It would be fair to say, though, that Paulhan had read more widely than most, even though his erudition is often well disguised by his celebrated modesty. Indeed, his better-known role as editor of the *Nouvelle Revue Française,* and as an extremely influential figure in the French publishing world, very much determined the range of writers that came into his line of vision. It also accounts for his approach to the activity of reading and writing, and his sense of how literature works, or does not work. His objective in packing his text so full of literary allusions was not simply an exercise in erudite name-dropping. The point he is making about literature is that one can observe certain invariant features across the infinite range of its historical manifestations, the constants which could allow one to formulate a quasi-scientific law of the literary act itself. In this sense Paulhan would want his text ultimately to mirror, or to mimic, the very timeless and universally applicable quality he finds in commonplace expressions, proverbs, maxims, literary clichés, and other hackneyed uses of language. *The Flowers of Tarbes,* which derives its central allegory of the "literary flowers" in the public park in Tarbes from the most well-worn of metaphors (the "garden" of literature), essentially offers itself to us with all the enigmatic doubleness of a cliché: are we to read it as a revelation of some immutable, eternal truth about literature, as an attempt to wrest some hitherto hidden secret from its depths? Or is it really nothing more than a soon-to-be outmoded running commentary on a series of already-outmoded views about literature which, like proverbs in their more banal and parochial guise, merely signal an attachment to *that* place, at *that* time? Although it may appear to be aimed at a specialist target audience, Paulhan's text engages with much broader questions. Paulhan attempts to identify, within the literature and criticism of the previous century and a half, a core set of fundamental beliefs about the way language works, which he then proceeds to interrogate with unremitting tenacity. His ensuing discussions of the nature of the act of literary creation, and the relationship between language, meaning, context, intention and action, are highly original, and extraordinarily prescient. This is a book that, like the public park in Tarbes, is open to everyone, and is at the same time a well-kept secret waiting to be discovered, or rediscovered.

In Which the Author Artfully Arranges His Flowers

The present text is a translation of the 1941 Gallimard edition of *Les fleurs de Tarbes,* its first publication as an independent volume. Paulhan had begun to compose his text as far back as 1925, when he first mentioned it in a letter to Francis Ponge. Several sections of the text were published, in modified form, in journals and anthologies between 1926 and 1938, and an earlier, shorter version of the text as a whole appeared in serial format in the *Nouvelle Revue Française* from June to October 1936. Paulhan promised a sequel to *The Flowers of Tarbes,* which he planned to call *Le don des langues* [The Gift of Languages], although he never in fact produced it.[1] The task of a genetic critic wanting to reconstruct the composition of this text is, however, potentially endless, since to those bits and pieces which are reproduced in some form, one would have to add almost the entirety of his oeuvre, which could be seen as one long and infinitely patient attempt to answer the same question: How do language and literature work? Or, as Maurice Blanchot would put it in the title of his famous essay on *The Flowers of Tarbes:* How is literature possible?[2]

It is worth reflecting for a moment on the nuts and bolts of the construction of *The Flowers of Tarbes.* The text itself has a pleasingly symmetrical arrangement of chapters and sub-sections, but the narrative itself is anything but polished and seamless. It has the feel, instead, of an ongoing work in progress, something put together by an amateur craftsman who is content for us to watch him as he proceeds, slowly and haltingly, through the trial and error of his labor. While much of the text consists of a rather loosely assembled collage of quotations from other writers, it also exemplifies the process of continuous *self-quotation* that marks Paulhan's writing more generally, where the same turns of phrase and stylistic tics, the same clichés, the same little illustrative tales, reappear in different guises and different contexts.[3] This is perhaps a necessary effect of his constant (and constantly thwarted) attempts to isolate specimens of language in order to show how language as a whole works. As he puts it, in one of the many proverbial formulations generated in the text, "Run away from language and it will come after you. Go after language and it will run away from you."[4] When this linguistic elusiveness is mapped onto the larger narrative sequences of the text, what happens is that the very process of narrating surprises the narrator, continually catching him unawares. His investigation ends up taking him in completely unexpected directions. As he says on the first page of *The Flowers of Tarbes:* "These are not the problems I was thinking of—far from it—when I undertook this study." He is ultimately, he admits, in no more privileged a position than we are to anticipate the outcome of his experiment. Likewise, if the text is read as a kind of *roman à clef,* based on the model of the mystery or detective novel Paulhan refers to at the end of *The Flowers of Tarbes,* it is unclear whether the "exemplary" little narratives which constantly interrupt the course of his investigation (the soldier on leave, the monk in Assisi who invents catastrophes in order to announce them, the butcher who takes years to "discover" how blood circulates, different methods of controlling mosquitoes, the public park in Tarbes, and so on) stand in a relationship of assured analogy or of uncertain contiguity to the main narrative.

There is certainly one historically determined reason why Paulhan's text gravitates toward those moments when language breaks down, or the inevitability of Terror falling victim to the Rhetoric it condemns. The period of Terror during the French Revolution is seen as a crucial marker of discontinuity, as if literary history itself had taken a traumatic wrong turn at some point around then, and as if one could return to that point of rupture to work out exactly what went wrong in the hope of repairing the rift. In *The Flowers of Tarbes,* though, the weight of this responsibility is borne with a disarming lightness of touch, and with characteristic irony and subtle humor. The chapter titles indeed consciously mimic a picaresque adventure novel ("In Which Terror is Not Entirely Implausible"), and hark back to an age when language and meaning were not so threatened, or threatening, and writers felt secure enough to revel in them freely. So how seriously are we to take Paulhan's text? Is it, after all, just a fanciful literary exercise ("... let's just say I have said nothing")? Or does it indeed achieve something of major importance, such as "The End of Terror in Literature," as the final words of the book performatively declare? Where does Paulhan ultimately situate himself with respect to Terror and Rhetoric?

Of Terror and Rhetoric

Rhetoric is, for Paulhan, based on the premise that language is essentially in no need of change. In an earlier text more explicitly concerned with rhetoric entitled *Traité des figures* [Treatise on Figures], a commentary on Dumarsais's *Traité des tropes* [Treatise on Tropes], Paulhan discussed the eighteenth century's obsession with classifying rhetorical figures and tropes, and saw the need to catalog figures in this way as consistent with the stability of rhetoric, which he associates with commonplace expressions, *lieux communs* (*lieu* in French being a more neutral and specifically linguistic term than "commonplace" in English). *The Flowers of Tarbes,* however, starts out by discussing an opposing tendency within literature, which Paulhan refers to as "Terror." Although the term is by the 1940s situated in a far broader philosophical context—that is, the French reception of Hegel's account of the dialectical unfolding of European history, with the French Revolution as the decisive "end" of this history—there is only one explicit reference in *The Flowers of Tarbes* to the period of Terror, represented by one of its most fanatical figures, Joseph Lebon:

> We call periods of *Terror* those moments in the history of nations (which often follow some famine), when it suddenly seems that the State requires not ingeniousness and systematic methods, nor even science and technology—no one cares about any of that—but rather an extreme purity of the soul, and the freshness of a communal innocence. Consequently citizens themselves are taken into consideration, rather than the things they do or make: The chair is forgotten in favor of the carpenter, the remedy in favor of the doctor. Skill, knowledge, and technique, however, become suspect, as if they were covering up some lack of conviction. (*Flowers,* 24)

Terror, then, stands not so much for the historical events themselves, but rather for a decisive turning point in French history, and more specifically in French *literary* history. This is described by Paulhan as a shift from the rule-bound imperatives of rhetoric and genre to the gradual abandonment of these rules in Romanticism and its successors, with the consequent search for greater originality of expression. This opposing imperative is what Paulhan terms *Terror.* Terrorist writers are those who demand continual invention and renewal, and denounce rhetoric's codification of language, its tendency to stultify the spirit and impoverish human experience. Paulhan finds examples of the Terrorist dismissal of rhetoric in, for example, Rémy de Gourmont's condemnation of "moral clichés," or Antoine Albalat's scorn for "picturesque clichés," or Flaubert's ironic dictionary of received ideas. In fact, everywhere he looks, Paulhan sees evidence of Terror in action: For Hyppolite Taine, Racine was "the epitome of verbalism" (*Flowers,* 28); for Renan the entire classical literary tradition was "an abuse of rhetoric" (*Flowers,* 28); and Brunetière discredited Malherbe's poetry for similar reasons. When Paulhan turns his attention to more contemporary examples, he comes across the (dangerously seductive) "power of words," and broadens his discussion beyond the realm of literature by including personal anecdotes, amusing little stories, and popular journalism (the clichés of the time being, for example, "ideological warfare," "the youth of today," "freedom," "popular opinion," and so on). Henri Bergson is seen by Paulhan as the supreme "anti-verbalist" critic of the first half of the twentieth century, and is described as Terror's own philosopher. Bergson's challenge to literature is "without doubt the most serious reproach made in our time: that the author of commonplace expressions gives in to the power of words, to verbalism, to the influence of language, and so on" (*Flowers,* 20).

The opposition between Terror and Rhetoric appears, then, to polarize two conflicting ideologies of expression, which seem to be mutually exclusive and irreconcilable: on the one hand the aspiration toward originality, and on the other the attraction to the stability of the commonplace, and this is seen by Paulhan as something that is a universal characteristic of literature and language, and not limited to any particular historical or cultural context. After he amply demonstrates the persuasive power of Terror's arguments, Paulhan proceeds to cast doubt on the validity of its philosophy: "Not that I find the mystical possession or the self-effacement of critics or scholars—nor, earlier in the text, the revolution—in the least bit contemptible. Far from it. I'm simply suspicious of a revolt, or a dispossession, which comes along so opportunely to get us out of trouble" (*Flowers,* 15). He then dismantles Terrorist claims by showing that they are the victims of an optical illusion: "These days when we come into contact with literature and with language, we are only able to know them, to appreciate them, and therefore also to continue them ourselves, thanks to a series of errors and illusions as crude as an optical illusion" (*Flowers,* 65). Terrorist writers are, as he shows, paradoxically enslaved to language, since they spend all their time trying to bypass it, or rid it of its clichés:

> For Terror is above all dependent upon language in a general sense, in that it condemns a writer to say only what a certain *state* of language leaves him free to express: He is restricted to those areas of feeling and thought where language has not yet been overused. That is not all: No writer is more preoccupied with words than the one who at every point sets out to get rid of them, to get away from them, or to reinvent them. (*Flowers,* 76)

Terror's "optical illusion," then, takes the form of a kind of blindness to its own rhetorical status. According to Paulhan, both Terrorists and Rhetoricians are justified in their conceptions of literature, and therefore are both equally unjustified. The problem is compounded in that the two "sides" in this exchange are in fact opposing perspectives on the *same* literary or linguistic object. What appears to some as verbalism ("just words") appears to others as authentic expressiveness (ideas or thoughts), and this becomes the central enigma of *The Flowers of Tarbes:* How is it possible to tell whether an author intended his or her words to be read as literary clichés or as original expressions? Commonplace expressions thus reveal a deep-seated tension within language and literature. They are "janus-faced" forms of language, as Blanchot puts it, which "subject the reader to equivocation."[5]

How does Paulhan attempt to resolve this tension? Paulhan's solution to the paradox is a revalorization (or a "reinvention") of rhetoric, a redoubled Rhetoric he will distinguish from the accepted understanding of the term by capitalizing it (and which he will also refer to as *Maintenance*). He suggests that writers should recognize clichés *as* clichés, and thereby establish a communally agreed-upon Rhetoric in order to remove the perplexing ambiguity that characterizes commonplace expressions:

> Clichés may once again take up residence in literature the day they are at last deprived of their ambiguity and their confusion. Now all it should require, since the confusion stems from a doubt as to their nature, is simply for us to *agree,* once and for all, to accept them as clichés. In short, we simply need to *make* commonplace expressions *common* . . . (*Flowers,* 79)

Blanchot compares this solution of a "reinvented" Rhetoric to a Copernican revolution, in which thought, if it is to rediscover its authenticity, needs to be controlled by the gravitational force field of language. This granting of a kind of residence permit to clichés allows them to re-enter literature, in that they become publicly acceptable and quotable, and are marked by a communally recognized citationality. Paulhan often sets apart such expressions *within* his text precisely by marking them with italics, and is aware of similar conventions in literature: "In terms of writing conventions, we should also mention the italics, the quotation marks and the parentheses, which we see proliferate in Romantic writers as soon as rhetoric is invalidated" (*Flowers,* 80n3).

The problems are far from over, though, since Paulhan's solution of a communally agreed acceptance of clichés is not the end of the book, which in fact closes with the surprising retraction: "There are thus glimmers of light, visible to whomever sees them, hidden from whomever looks at them; gestures which cannot be performed without a certain negligence . . . In fact, let's just say I have said nothing" (Flowers, 94). This seems at first to be an example of the kind of playfulness and modesty typical of Paulhan. It takes the form of a proposed mutual agreement ("let's just say") that is expressed as an optic metaphor. We can no more fully comprehend the solution than we can look squarely at the sun, and the negligence he suggests could be described as the passivity involved in just seeing, as opposed to the effort involved in looking. The ending seems to be an example of this kind of negligence. However, this disavowal casts doubt on our very ability to come to any decisive judgment, or in short, to read: in Paulhan's own terms, this final sentence is strictly undecidable or unreadable. What we are left with is no longer simply a rather intriguing theory about literature, because in submitting his own language to the same uncertainty or undecidability, the whole book is put into question. The book is thus a performance of the very radical ambiguity that it talks about, an ambiguity which is not simply an equivocation about *what* the book is saying, but which suspends it between saying and doing, stating and performing, original and commonplace.

How Reading This Book Could Change Your Life

Paulhan's concern, though, is to find a way to *keep language working*, in spite of its inherent tensions and endless aporias. Indeed, his efforts to establish a common and more fully-inclusive agreement that would cover all words and expressions reflect a deeper anxiety about our capacity to function together effectively as a society, or to form something like a consensual democracy.[6] While he was critical of the notion of politically-committed literature that dominated the post-war literary scene in France, he certainly did not follow Blanchot and others in divorcing literature from any immediate social relevance, even though this was a prevalent misconception about Paulhan, particularly in light of his defense of collaborationist writers after the Second World War. One of the powerful undercurrents of his thinking, which is continually reinforced by the constant recourse to a legalistic terminology in *The Flowers of Tarbes* (finding evidence, being on trial, seeing justice is done, passing sentence, and so on), is for language and literature to somehow recover their ethical responsibility, a concern that is foregrounded early on in the text: "We have, to all intents and purposes, given up on knowing what literature *owes* us" (*Flowers,* 2). In this respect he is perhaps close to Jacques Derrida, especially the latter's recent work on democracy, justice, chance, hospitality, and the openness to the other in thinking through the implications of performative effects in language. Indeed, Paulhan's argument about "the power of words" in many ways anticipates Derrida's early critique of speech act theory. It might be said that Paulhan's use of Rhetoric "against" Terror involves a very similar reversal to the one Derrida brings into play in "Signature event context," his reading of J. L. Austin's philosophy of performative language (and later in his reply to John Searle in "Limited Inc.").[7] The thrust of Derrida's deconstruction of the concept of pure, successful or "felicitous" performatives (and the corresponding unsuccessful, improper, or "infelicitous" instances they are anxious to exclude from their theories), is to argue that the priority of purity/impurity, or original/secondary, should be the other way around. What he means is that "pure" performatives are always *already* contaminated or infected by a prior and necessary impurity, insofar as they are open to the possibility that they might not perform, or do what they say they are going to do. In typically deconstructive style, Derrida shows how performative language requires a principle of *iterability* in order to function, and I would see this as akin to Paulhan's insistence on the citationality of a "reinvented" Rhetoric. Just as Derrida stresses that he is not denying that there *are* instances of successful performatives, so Paulhan is concerned to safeguard language (and by extension literature, politics, ethics, and history).

If *The Flowers of Tarbes* revels in drawing attention to slippages of language, including its own, and to the essential undecidability between the constative and performative functions of language, it is anxious at the same time to stabilize these slippages. As we saw, if Revolution and Terror meant the loss of a sovereign, unifying power, then this brought with it the corresponding loss of a stable linguistic system. What Paulhan is trying to do beyond simply narrating this loss, and cataloguing its effects, is to secure the means of protecting language from constantly falling back into the same abyss into which it has collapsed, or of falling back into the same illusions it is denouncing. This is the crux of his argument about "the power of words." This was not his term, but was the title of a regular column before the Second World War in the journal *Les Nouveaux Cahiers*. Contributors to the column included influential contemporary writers and intellectuals, such as Brice Parain, Denis de Rougemont, and Simone Weil. Their intention was to awaken readers to the dangers of how terms in common political currency, such as "democracy," "class," "war," "violence," and so on, were being misused, but with the idea that these terms could be made to signify correctly if we were more careful in applying them correctly. Paulhan's point was that consensual agreement cannot be achieved by stabilizing meaning once and for all, since this would merely imply reasserting the power of some new repressive force (like that of a monarch), or having one's freedom similarly constrained by the imposition of rhetorical rules and codes. Cementing the relationship between language, intention, and action would be in effect to elide the distinction between performative and constative language.[8] While Paulhan is keen to establish something similar to a consensually agreed upon legislation about performative language, his argument is that if there is no allowance made for slippages of meaning, for performatives misfiring, for interruptions in communication, and the like, then abuses of linguistic power will continue to operate unchallenged.

Again, this is a way of understanding the relationship of a performative utterance to its context which is close to Derrida's in "Limited Inc." As J. Hillis Miller puts it in his commentary on Derrida's text:

The context is there already, but it becomes a context only when the speech act intervenes within it, however weakly and without power to saturate it. The speech act nevertheless transforms the context it enters, even though in retrospect that context seems to have been there already as the ground of the speech act's efficacy. This power to intervene in the context, even if not to dominate it, is the emancipatory chance opened by a speech-act theory based on iterability.[9]

There is thus a certain necessary contingency about how language works, how it enters the context in which it performs, and how it tranforms this context, all the while giving the appearance that this context preceded it as its ground or frame. *The Flowers of Tarbes* relates performative language and ethics in a similar way, and the text could be read as a sustained effort on Paulhan's part to articulate something like an ethical imperative of language and literature. A deliberate openness to unpredictable contingency is what Derrida has more recently theorized as hospitality, and as certain unconditional laws of justice and democracy. "Reading" *The Flowers of Tarbes* is thus more and less than understanding cognitively the twists and turns of Paulhan's unsettling arguments. It is only once we begin to respond to the text's performative self-awareness that we can be said to begin to read it, but by then we are already on very slippery ground, especially since the book challenges fundamentally what we thought we understood to be the ground we were standing on. Reading (and, *a fortiori,* translating!) *The Flowers of Tarbes* in fact involves abandoning the illusion of any meta-narrative security from the text and the linguistic tensions it grapples with, but by accepting the terms of the book's contract with us, by entering into its contexts, and participating in its transformation, we are at the same time altered or transformed.

A Few Words on Translating Paulhan

Jean Paulhan has a singular French prose style, full of subtle wit and playful irony. Although humor is a matter of personal taste, and does not always travel well, this is a text that is at times very funny, and I sincerely hope that not too much of this is lost in translation. It was a formidable challenge when translating this text to match Paulhan's combination of an informal, casual, even conversational tone, and his extremely erudite references, or to capture the graceful ease with which he elaborates his ideas, but at the same time the quirky contours of his rather awkward, discontinuous syntax. To stay too close to the original, of course, is to run the risk of coming across simply as poor translation, but to render it more fluent in English than it is in French would be to ignore the unique qualities of Paulhan's style. I have tried to guide the English carefully through this narrow strait, and tidied it up only where necessary for minimal intelligibility. So the reader can be forewarned that stylistic features such as ellipsis and anacoluthon, anaphora and other repetitive sequences, sudden interjections, unannounced shifts from direct to indirect discourse, a blurring of his narrative voice within the fictionalized apostrophes to the many writers he is in dialogue with, and inconsistent punctuation, are all there (intentionally or not) in the original. Another problematic consideration is the question of gender. Whenever Paulhan refers to writers, critics, or readers in a generic sense, it is always masculine in French. The initial temptation is to assume his usage is not intentionally gender-exclusive, and to try to correct it accordingly so as to produce a more gender-inclusive English text. It very soon becomes apparent that this is not only unworkable in practice, since it would bear too heavily on the language of the text, but it would also be something of a cultural distortion. One has to simply accept that the literary world in France at that time was a largely masculine domain, and that when Paulhan was thinking about writers, he probably was thinking almost exclusively of male writers.

Apart from the difficulty of conveying adequately the elusive quality of his style and tone, there is one other strictly untranslatable feature that goes to the very core of what *The Flowers of Tarbes* is saying: clichés and commonplace expressions. Anyone who speaks another language knows that clichés, proverbs, idioms, commonplace expressions, and so on, are all highly resistant to translation, since they are those parts of language that are most linguistically and culturally specific. Paulhan himself was well aware of this, having translated an anthology of proverbs from Malagasy to French, as well as having reflected at length on his difficulties in learning Malagasy proverbs and applying them successfully. As he points outs, clichés and proverbial language always strike us as more colorful and imaginative in a foreign language than in our own, so translation always brings to the fore precisely the point he is making about the conflicting but equally valid dual perspectives of Rhetoric and Terror. One passage where this is evident is the discussion, in the section "In Which the Author Uses a Cliché," of Paul Bourget's and Francis Carco's hackneyed phrases, which Paulhan highlights in order to show how metaphors and figures of speech are distorted and lose the original force of their meaning over time. He points out that *any* phrase can potentially solidify into a set sequence of words, such as "mysterious-languor" or a "habit-which-governs." Clichés thus occur, according to Paulhan, whenever semantics shades over into syntax in this way, when the mechanical aspect of language overrides its meaning aspect. A lot of the time a translated cliché can hold its own *as a cliché* in another linguistic or literary cultural context, but when I have felt it clearly does not, I have retained the French in parentheses, particularly when Paulhan plays on the French word or expression itself. So the work of translation remains intentionally visible, and this mirrors the way in which Paulhan himself constantly draws attention to the composition of his text. Both processes are essentially engaged with the same questions of reading and writing, of trying to determine linguistic effect or performative force, and ultimately giving in to a certain mechanical necessity of language, which is not in any sense an admission of failure. If anything, translation participates fully in the kind of reading that the text invites us to engage in, a reading that is ethically responsible precisely to the extent that, to borrow Paulhan's phrase, we "yield to its imperatives" (*Flowers*, 69).

Notes

1. The earlier avatars of what would become *Les fleurs de Tarbes* are "Défaut de langage," *Anthologie de la nouvelle prose française* (Editions du Sagittaire, 1926); "Sur un défaut de la pensée critique," *Commerce* 16 (summer 1928); "Commentaire sur Bruno Latini," *Mesures* (15 January 1937); "Lettre aux *Nouveaux Cahiers* sur le pouvoir des mots," *Les Nouveaux Cahiers* 22, 23–24, 25); "Le secret de la critique," *Mesures* (15 juillet 1938); and "Éléments," *Mesures* (15 octobre 1938). Paulhan did publish a text called *Le don des langues* towards the end of his life, but this should not be confused with his promised "conclusion" to *Les fleurs de Tarbes.* He added several notes and documents to the main body of *The Flowers of Tarbes,* which were intended to provide further proof and illustration of his ideas. I chose not to translate these in the interests of containing and identifying the main project called *The Flowers of Tarbes.* Interested readers are referred to the 1990 Folio edition of *Les fleurs de Tarbes,* edited by Jean-Claude Zylberstein, which gathers together many of the above texts in a very useful appendix.

2. "Comment la littérature est-elle possible?" *Journal des débats,* 7 Dec. 1941, reprinted in *Faux Pas* (Paris: Gallimard, 1943). Translated into English by Michael Syrotinski as "How Is Literature Possible?" in Michael Holland, ed. *The Blanchot Reader* (Oxford: Blackwell, 1995), 49–60. For a fuller discussion of this article and its resonances, see the chapter "Blanchot Reading Paulhan" in Michael Syrotinski, *Defying Gravity* (Albany, N.Y.: SUNY Press, 1998), 77–104.

3. In the "Notes and Documents" to *Les fleurs de Tarbes,* Paulhan literally includes a quotation by himself in a long list of contradictory opinions about the same novel. Following his example, I have included a brief biography of Paulhan in the "Names Mentioned" section.

4. *The Flowers of Tarbes*, 82. References are all to the present translation, and will be given subsequently with the abbreviated title *Flowers*, followed by the page number in parentheses.

5. Blanchot, "How Is Literature Possible?" 52.

6. The political implications of this position, particularly in terms of his highly original thinking about the concept of democracy, will be developed more extensively in his post-war texts on the literary purge, such as *Of Wheat and Chaff* (trans. Richard Rand, University of Illinois Press, 2004). Anna-Louise Milne performs an excellent analysis of *The Flowers of Tarbes* along these lines in her monograph on Paulhan, *The Extreme In-Between (Politics and Literature): Jean Paulhan's Place in the Twentieth Century* (Oxford: Legenda, forthcoming).

7. Jacques Derrida, "Signature Event Context" and "Limited Inc.," trans. Samuel Weber and Jeffrey Mehlman (Evanston, Ill.: Northwestern University Press, 1988).

8. Anna-Louise Milne, in her study *The Extreme In-Between*, demonstrates how this dynamic echoes Judith Butler's thinking around the question of speech acts in political discourse, *Excitable Speech: A Politics of the Performative* (London and New York: Routledge, 1997), and the problems inherent in attempts to legislate against certain injurious acts of language, for example, hate speech, racist slander, pornography, and so on. Butler demonstrates the danger of placing faith in the apparent neutrality of a law as a means of sanctioning against offensive language, if such laws are imagined to replace the function of a kind of sovereign power, since the "law," in a Foucauldian sense, is anything but discursively neutral.

9. J. Hillis Miller, *Speech Acts in Literature* (Stanford, Calif.: Stanford University Press, 2001), 111.

The Flowers of Tarbes
or, Terror in Literature

For André Gide

❦ ❦ ❦   *People happily talk about the mystery of poetry and of literature. They talk about it ad nauseam. However, nothing is explained, I have to confess, by alluding here to magic or religious ecstasy, wishing stones or observant animals. To talk about the ineffable is to say precisely nothing at all. To talk about secrets is to confess nothing. Poets may indeed be devout, but to what are they devoted? Writers may know a great deal, but what kind of knowledge is it?*

It is up to the poet or novelist to decide whether he is happy with this deplorable confusion. If he has an experience of mystery, and spreads it around, it's not his business to explain it. He may in fact convey it all the better by refusing himself to it. But there is another kind of writer whose task it is to remind us tirelessly what this mystery is all about, and who seems lost.

It would appear, strangely, that critics these days have given up their prerogative and abandoned their right to scrutinize literature. They are supposed to lay down the law. But instead they now lose their way in expressions of fatuous reverence. "Let the creators begin!" they say. Or "What can I do on my own?" They ask only that they be allowed to look on and keep their accounts (but that too will be taken away from them).

These are not the problems I was thinking of—far from it—when I undertook this study. It would have seemed vain and pretentious of me to tackle them. In fact literature these days deals with a thousand more urgent issues, such as poverty, solitude, or excess.

I

A Portrait of Terror

CHAPTER 1

❦ ❦ ❦ Literature in Its Wild State

> As I was about to repeat the words that this kind native woman taught me, she shouted out: "Stop! Each one can only be used once . . ."
> —Botzarro's Travel Journal, XV

There are few events in literature that we are likely to find enchanting. This in itself is perhaps not surprising, but it seems that we are from the outset not even allowing ourselves to be enchanted. Beauty means little more to us than a reason to feel wary. Some say that polished works of literature are indifferent, while others say that a subject is dangerous because of its beauty. And there are those, finally, for whom nothing resembles mediocrity as much as perfection. I am merely citing the most erudite critics.[1] "Beautiful lines of poetry are forbidden," Hugo once said.

We are left then with a work's character, and its ability to surprise us. Yet here again, literature immediately snatches away the very thing it appears to be giving us. No sooner are we familiar with the character of a work than it becomes mechanical, and once we are used to its way of surprising us, it is the opposite of a surprise. Péguy contends that a writer produces one authentic work of literature, then spends the rest of his life imitating himself. Gourmont adds that a personal work quickly becomes obscure if it is a failure, banal if it is a success, and discouraging in any event. So beauty starts out by disappointing us, and character ends up by doing so. There is not much difference

---

1. Cf. Jouffroy (*Pensées*), Edmond Jaloux (*Nouvelles littéraires,* 7 September 1929), and André Maurois (*Bravo,* 15 January 1930). "Why are perfect writers not great writers?" Victor Hugo asked (*Post-Scriptum de ma vie*).

between the two. We have, to all intents and purposes, given up on knowing what literature *owes* us. We are thrown before it, defenseless and without any method for proceeding, completely disoriented.

This is not for lack of hopes or aspirations.

For Every Great Hope There Is a Great Disappointment

Victor Hugo thought of himself as a pope, Lamartine a statesman, and Barrès a general. Paul Valéry expects to get from literature what a philosopher doesn't always dare to hope from philosophy: He wants to know what man is capable of. And Gide, to know what man is.

All Claudel believes we need to do is to rebuild the sacred world we had in the Middle Ages upon the ruins of secular society. Breton, however, insists upon the triumph of a new ethics based on crime and magic. "Poetry has ways of doing this," he says, "whose effectiveness we underestimate." Maurras seems to think it is sufficient, but necessary, for a writer to hold above water the head of an entire sinking civilization. And I'll say nothing of Alerte, for whom poetry seems so serious that he has taken the decision to stop writing it.

I do not know if it is true that men of letters were at one time content just to entertain high society. (So they said at any rate.) Even the most modest among us expect literature to reveal at last a religion, a moral code, and the meaning of life. There's not a single pleasure of the mind that literature doesn't owe them. And who, a young man asks, could stand not to be a writer?

What? Who says literature is equipped to deal with such subjects? "I didn't say it dealt with them." So why does it address them? What is the point of discussing them? "I have no idea. It may be that people are expecting more. It may also be that literature has become less generous. It is as if literature used to be the place where free, and joyous, and perhaps slightly insane things happened, but we have lost all memory, and even the very idea, of these things. No longer knowing exactly what benefit it ought to bring us, we begin by demanding everything of it. (Just as one sues for a hundred thousand francs in order to get fifty.)"

That would be the easiest way of being disappointed. "You're right, we are disappointed."

You don't need to look too far to find what prevents Rimbaud from thinking highly of himself. It is the poem he has just written. No sooner has Paul Valéry passed a decisive judgment on the poet, his methods, and the forces that motivate his work, than he apologizes and appears unsure of himself. Should he be the one who dares to make such a verdict? No. He does not want to prevent anyone from writing. Fantasies are only worth something to those who write, he says, out of weakness.

Claudel decrees and judges, but not without letting God, nature, or the stars intervene. "This revolting book . . ." "But your criticism . . .," people tell him. "My criticism! Do you take me for a stablehand?" "But your work . . ." ". . . a man of letters is a prostitute!"

Who would expect reasonable thinking from Aragon? His job is to charm us, and to make us dream. Rostand is clumsy compared to him. But Aragon calls literature a machine that turns people into morons, and calls men of letters crabs. If he is not a crab, one wonders what there is left for him.

I am talking about the best there are. How do we make them understand they are writing? "I'm not, at any rate, doing it deliberately," Arland replies. Yet many writers, from Balzac to Proust, apologize for characters who, it seems, urge these writers to bring them to life. Apollinaire would certainly prefer perfumes, noises, or lines to these disagreeable words. It seems, when all is said and done, that one cannot be a decent writer if one is not disgusted by literature. Just as there is no revelation that literature is not expected to provide, so there is no contempt it does not also seem to deserve. And every young writer is astonished that anyone can stand to be a writer. Almost the only way we can manage to talk about novels, style, literature, or art is by using ruses, or new words, which do not yet seem offensive. If there is such a thing as a happy experience, it evaporates, and no indication or sign of it remains. And nothing happens, finally, that does not also happen the other way round in our literature, which is deprived of memory and as if still in a wild state.

This misunderstanding takes some unusual forms.

Where Critical Thinking Goes Wrong

Everyone knows that there are two kinds of literature these days: bad literature, which is quite unreadable (so everyone reads it). And good literature, which no one reads. This is what has been called, among other things, the separation of the writer from the public.

The famous library of the Dukes of Brécé, which had acquired all the great books of the 18th century, only took in works by Chateaubriand, Guizot, and Marchangy between 1800 and 1850.[2] After 1850, two or three pamphlets relating to Pope Pius XI, and a panegyric of Joan of Arc. This was very little. According to Charles Maurras, this was not the fault of the Dukes of Brécé, but of the writers themselves, of their anarchic declarations as much as of their abstruse cryptograms, which respectable society found not in the slightest bit appealing or interesting; there was nothing about them that it felt duty-bound to encourage.

This may well be true. Yet there is no enigma or cryptogram, as far as I can see—be it anarchic or revolutionary—which does not at first have the support of the most respectable society. Arcane reviews are printed on very fine paper; things you read on candle paper are always sensible and very clear. And the Dukes of Brécé are famous today for their collections of Sade's manuscripts and of Surrealist invectives. But the separation is actually more serious than Maurras claims, and it is not only the aristocracy, but the bourgeoisie and the working class who, for the last hundred years or so, have been reading and admiring Feuillet, and not Flaubert; Gustave Droz, and not Bloy; Jean Aicard, and not Charles Cros; Madame de Noailles rather than Mallarmé; and Guy de Pourtalès rather than Marcel Jouhandeau. What do you expect if critics are the first to abandon and betray literature?

The nineteenth century has sometimes been referred to as the century of criticism. Ironically, no doubt; it was the century when any good critic *misunderstood* the writers of his time. Fontanes and Planche inveighed against Lamartine; and Nisard against Victor Hugo. We can-

---

2. See Anatole France, *L'Anneau d'améthyste*.

not read what Sainte-Beuve wrote about Balzac and Baudelaire without feeling ashamed; nor what Brunetière wrote about Stendhal and Flaubert; Lemaître about Verlaine or Mallarmé; Faguet about Nerval and Zola; Lasserre about Proust and Claudel. When Taine wanted to name a great novelist, he chose Hector Malot; Anatole France's idea of a great poet was Frédéric Plessis. They all, it goes without saying, completely ignored Cros, Rimbaud, Villiers, and Lautréamont. Malot, however, excelled at portraits, and Plessis at depicting unusual characters. The latter writes Essays, the former writes charming Journeys (in his books). The one literary genre that is closed to them is the one they lay claim to. If it is true that criticism is the counterpart to the literary arts, and in a sense their conscience, we have to admit that literature these days does not have a clear conscience.

It is not because of any lack of knowledge or of critical doctrines. Scholars have done their best. Some see the writer as the point of convergence of a people, an environment, and a moment in time. For others, the work of art is a game. Or then again, it is seen as a kind of carapace which man uses to shelter his desires. I won't even mention those who call it generously, but rather vaguely, an illumination, the union with the soul of things, and so on. The most sensible scholars recommend that if we want to understand literature, we should wait until it has stopped changing, and living.

However diverse these doctrines are, they have two things in common. The first is their uselessness: We have never seen any writer foolish enough to try to live up to the image that Taine, Spencer, or Freud form of the writer. The second thing is the modesty of these doctrines: They readily accept that they are of no use.

Pierre Audiat commented recently that serious critics (among whom he counts himself) gave up judging novels or poems a long time ago. No doubt. And perhaps even *thinking about* them. Sainte-Beuve attempted to classify writers' minds; their works seemed inconsequential to him. He identified the effect a wrinkle has on a poem, not the effect a poem has on a wrinkle. Taine and Freud, obsessed with causes and effects, only study the work, they say, in order to understand the man. Brunetière maintains, bizarrely, that *Le Cid* is to some extent a work by Corneille, but that it is to a far greater extent the work of Richelieu,

Chapelain, and public opinion. A critic is free to be a historian or a psychologist. However, the author eludes us if his work does; and the man if the author does.

A Man Rendered Speechless

I have talked about literature. I might just as well be talking about language: discussions, things shouted out, confessions, tales told of an evening. I have said, and everyone knows, that Sainte-Beuve misunderstood Baudelaire. But it is no less true (although it is less well-known) that my neighbor Monsieur Bazot gets confused when talking to his maid, and all muddled by the—somewhat mysterious—explanations of his gardener. The malady affecting literature would, after all, be fairly insignificant if it didn't reveal a chronic illness of expression in general.

This is to say nothing of a world in which political leaders talk Peace when they are thinking War; Order when they are thinking Slaughter; and Nobility, Devotion, and Chivalry when they are thinking God knows what. You may tell me in their defense that it's all a strategy, and that the greatness of a political leader can be measured by his contempt for the poor little words we all use.[3] But political leaders are not that malicious, nor ordinary folk that naïve. I would be surprised if words didn't have something to say on the matter. I know that they often fail me. And not only words. Ordinary people have the right to say what they think at all times. Or even to sing it. Or even to put it into images. But we have given up these rights a long time ago.

I am not only thinking of the systems of drawings and diagrams—lines, triangles, spirals—that we sometimes imagine we have inside ourselves, and which shift and change according to how our various enterprises develop and progress. But also of the myriad private fantasies that enter our minds, and often obsess us, before disappearing. I remember, not without some embarrassment, having been tormented

---

3. Mr. Molotov, the Soviet Foreign Minister, noted in one of his most recent speeches (March 1940) that the word *aggression* had just changed its meaning, "now that events have given it a new historical content that is the opposite of its former one."

for a time by a certain feeling, precise but hard to define, and which would have been best expressed by the image of a little man, submerged and lost at the bottom of an aquarium. Now I have never in fact drawn that image. Instead I will talk about something more general, what one might call the *silence of the soldier on leave*. Everyone knows that when soldiers came home on leave in 1914 they did not talk, a fact that pacifist propaganda used to great effect. They saw this silence as being caused on the one hand by the horrors of war, which were literally unspeakable, and on the other by the unwillingness of the soldier's family, who would have refused to understand in any case. In short they took as the motivation for this silence the two reasons which normally prompt a man to speak (and even to chatter on and on): the unusual nature of what he has to say, and the difficulty he has convincing his mother or wife. The right thing to do would have been to interpret this silence as the great mystery, and the paradox, of war. But these were the rules, and the soldiers never *recognized* themselves in the works that attempted to depict what they were doing. It was as if every man were mysteriously afflicted by an illness of language.

Of language and of literature, for the one does not go without the other. Not only in books, but in conversation as well, perfection is a cause for concern: "Too eloquent to be sincere," we think, and "Too nicely put to be true."

There is not a single thought, even the subtlest, which does not also seem to call for its expression. But there is not a single expression which does not seem willfully deceptive or false. When people talk about "sayings" and "words," it is in order to bemoan all that they remain incapable of conveying, the most precious thing about us, if we are to believe what they say. So we do have to admit that we have trouble understanding one another!

Nonetheless, it seems that nothing on earth will make us renounce so much disappointment. Lawrence, who aspires to get as close as possible to humanity, bitterly compares his worldly success with his human failure. Likewise, the man in the street finds that he is unable to get in touch with other people. What am I saying, with other people! With himself, if it is indeed true that any feeling, in order to exist, has to be talked over with oneself. Even feelings about revolution and searching for God. Who would not be willing to see literature left to its own fate? But thought itself is then also compromised. We only wanted to kill off artists, but we end up beheading all men.

⚘ ⚘ ⚘   However odd and untamed literature and language appear to us, they just keep on going, and it is not without reason that they have been compared to honey, which bees make apparently without thinking about it. Literature and language are not, though, left as much to their own fate as one might think. They do incorporate their own recipes (not the least of which is the apparent absence of any recipe), and—to the more attentive observer—their own arguments and proofs.

If we pursue our investigation further in this direction, and try—naïvely and without reading between the lines—to tease apart the impressions upon which our sense of the literary is based, the immediate opinions that poets and literary critics use to support their arguments, and finally the answers that we give rather confusedly to this childish question "What is literature?"—childish, but which we spend our whole lives avoiding—then what we discern quite quickly, in amongst a mass of eulogies and reproaches, a collection of some things vaguely allowed and others definitely banned, is one very striking and central concern, which seems in a curious way to stand out on its own, and to cover itself with a kind of protective armor of reason. It would be foolish to let it go before it has given up its secret.

CHAPTER 2

✿ ✿ ✿ Poverty and Hunger

> No sooner had I arrived at Sainte-Beuve's than I
> began reading *Louisa*. After half an hour Sainte-Beuve
> exclaimed: "That is not a novel." I was about to burst
> into tears when he added, in the same tone of voice:
> "It is life itself."
> —The Memoirs of Thérèse Thirion, II, 8

Literature has probably always courted danger. Hölderlin went mad, Nerval hanged himself, Homer was blind his whole life. It seems that at the very moment a discovery is made that is going to change the shape of the world, every poet sees himself, like Columbus, clinging to his mast and risking death. I know of no dangers that are more insidious, nor any curses crueller, than those which belong to a time when *mastery* and *perfection* more or less denote artificiality and empty convention, when *beauty, virtuosity,* and even *literature* signify above all *what one must not do.*

A sign at the entrance to the Tarbes public park reads as follows:

> IT IS FORBIDDEN TO ENTER THE PARK
> CARRYING FLOWERS

The same sign can be found these days at the entrance to literature. How nice it would be, though, to see the young girls of Tarbes (and young writers) carrying a rose, a poppy, a bouquet of poppies.

The Break with Commonplace Expressions

Rhetoricians—at a time when there were books on rhetoric—used to explain obligingly how to write poetry; the sounds and words, the stylistic devices, and which rhetorical flowers one should use. Modern rhetoric, however, which it must be said is more diffuse and less explicit, but all the more forceful and stubborn, starts out by telling us which stylistic devices, sounds, and rules are apt to frighten poetry away for good. The literary arts are these days marked by refusal. There was a time when it was poetic to say *waters, wingèd chariot,* and *eventide.* But today it is poetic not to say *waters, wingèd chariot,* and *eventide.* It is better to steer clear of starry skies and precious stones. Do not write *calm lake,* says Sainte-Beuve, but *blue lake* instead, not *delicate fingers,* but *tapering fingers* instead. It may once have been desirable, but it is now forbidden, to say of voluptuousness that it is sweet, effeminate, or playful; of eyes that they are sparkling, eloquent, or melting. (And yet what if they are?). If we were to define writers over the last one hundred and fifty years, through their countless adventures, in terms of what they have always demanded, we find that they are unanimous in wanting to *refuse* something: so we have Rimbaud's "poetic old-fashionedness," Verlaine's "eloquence," or Victor Hugo's "rhetoric." "I had a lot of trouble," said Walt Whitman, "taking out all of the poetic traits from *Leaves of Grass,* but I managed it in the end." And according to Laforgue: "The hallowed culture of the future is an anti-culture." Jules Renard remarks that "The art of writing today lies in mistrusting worn-out words."

No doubt: and in bygone days it involved trusting words that were allowed, that had been used before, that were tried and tested. Now, these words are more or less the same. This former trust, and present mistrust, which seem to occupy the same place and weigh exactly the same, also share the same object—it is as if the entire mystery of literature came down to a single problem, whose solution could, depending on how we approached it, be completely different.

Or at any rate, if not its mystery, then those parts of it which can be regulated, manipulated, and crafted, since rules and genres follow clichés into exile. The first thing anyone attempting to write the history of poetry, of theatre, or of the novel over the last hundred years will find is that technique has slowly fallen away and detached itself from these genres. Secondly, that this technique has lost its own re-sources, and has been invaded by the secrets and processes of neighboring techniques—poetry by prose, the novel by lyricism, theatre by the novel. Maupassant said naïvely that the critic (and the novelist) should "search for anything that least resembles novels that have already been written." And the same goes for the other genres. Such that the theatre can find nothing it would like to avoid more than the theatrical, novels nothing more than the novelistic, and poetry nothing more than the poetic. And literature in general wishes to avoid nothing more than the literary. "It reads so much like a novel sometimes," Sainte-Beuve said (maliciously) about *Indiana.* "It's so theatrical," Jules Lemaître sighed in talking about *La Dame aux Camélias,* not without disdain.[1]

I'm not saying that novels or literature are wrong. I've no idea whether they are or not. And deprivation seems to me (as it does to everyone) desirable and even necessary. Indeed, I feel that any work which claims to be able to do without deprivation is quite mediocre. But I would not go so far as to say it is pleasing. It is no doubt the remedy that the corruption of our language or our thought requires. But it is a remedy that leaves a bad taste in the mouth. There's something humiliating about seeing words that have long charmed us being withdrawn, without getting anything back in return; and things along with words—because stones really are precious sometimes, just as fingers are sometimes delicate. We only wanted to break free from a language that was too conventional and now we are close to breaking free from all human language. Ancient poets took proverbs, clichés, and common feelings from all over the place. They welcomed this abundance, and gave it back in kind. But we who do not have much are in danger, at any moment, of losing the little we have. It is indeed a question of flowers! Horace said that commonplace expressions are the staple diet of our literature. What I would say to anyone who expresses surprise that more than one writer has turned to writing about morality, business, or politics is that they are fleeing like emigrants because they have nothing left to eat. And it is not without good reason that we canonized Rimbaud who stopped writing—and indeed emigrated—at the age of twenty.

---

1. Meaning the play, of course.

A First Alibi: The Author Is Different

I do not know if one should continue to write. Many excellent minds have questioned whether one should. Marcel Schwob was close to believing, and before him Renan, that the efforts of generations of Classical and Romantic writers left just one area to explore, this being the literature of erudition. Every line of poetry, said Fontanes, has already been written. Writers who persist in spite of everything, and do not want to give up, find several ways of getting around the problem.

The simplest one consists in describing feelings or presenting characters that are so out of the ordinary that commonplace expressions would be inappropriate for them, feelings and characters that are so complex that an entirely new language would be needed for them, one that made no prior allowance for them. We know too the uncompromising demand for originality which is at the present time the guiding principle of literature, and even of the choice of subject matter (which in the past sometimes derived its value from its banality). We need in any case to be able to discern a single leaf on a branch, or the baroque character of a man. Keep looking at a tree, Flaubert said, until you notice what is different about it. Or then again a writer will try to be so originally personal that he can only see or say things which are completely unexpected. "I don't have a style," both Wilde and Cocteau said. "I *am* a style." Which means that one can hardly make good literature out of good feelings any more,[2] nor put virtue into a poetic form. Fortunately the honest reader's resilience ensures that in this respect some monsters have a more durable novelty, and a kind of literary *advance*. The poetic value of a prostitute, of incest, of a rogue, or a homosexual has become a byword or a kind of model in literature, and without them many a novel or poem would remain obscure for us. (Do we need to point out that this situation is no less discourteous for the rogue or the homosexual than it is for the novelist?)

A durable novelty, to be sure, but not an eternal one. Writers today, at

---

2. Good feelings being those that one admits (or at least pretends to admit) are common.

least if they are scrupulous and want to remain credible, see themselves ultimately as being too directly interested in revolt, and in any kind of upheaval that might compel man and the world to renewal, for them not to be revolutionaries in secret, even if they dare not be overtly. But the distaste for clichés then turns into a hatred for contemporary society and ordinary feelings. As if Nation States and nature were not altogether different from some vast language that everyone spoke silently to themselves.

There is a more immediate form of originality that is related less to the subject of a work than to its expression. The Goncourts, Huysmans, Loti, with varying degrees of success all use a style that is constantly changing, that is a kind of "unwriting" (or at least that is how they would like it to be). Writers, however, are quick to observe that in this sense there are hardly any words or phrases that do not lend themselves to commonplace expressions. For there is a kind of contagiousness about clichés. No sooner has a poet dispensed with *starry skies* than he has to wonder about the *sky* and about *stars,* which are apt to bring the expression back to mind, and which already retain it as a rather unpleasant and dull reflection. Mallarmé had grave concerns about the moon, and finally decided to give it up. If *playful voluptuousness* is guilty, I am not so sure that *voluptuousness* will remain innocent for long. *Valley* suggests *delightful valley.* So one after another, every word is potentially suspect if it has already been used, as is every utterance, if its clarity is derived from commonplace expressions. Another hidden trend in literature—hidden, but from which have emerged some of the most enduring works ever seen in our time—demands of the poet, through some alchemy, *another* syntax, a new grammar, even forbidden words in which a sort of primitive innocence would come back to life, and some long lost adherence of language to the things in the world. This was the ambition, and sometimes the achievement, of Rimbaud, Apollinaire, Joyce. A not insignificant modern school[3] says that the first duty of a writer is to "dissociate matter from sentences";

---

3. This is the *Words-in-Freedom* school, whose leader was Marinetti.

another school suggests he should dissociate matter from words.[4] One individual thinker, Monsieur Hiliase, has gone as far as to take letters apart: his work is odd to look at—and even to feel, since the new letters he uses are presented in relief.

Another Alibi: The Author Is Irresponsible

One suspects other forms of self-defense or escape; those expressed in many a declaration found, unsurprisingly, at the beginning of a poem or a novel (and God knows how intent authors are on justifying themselves these days—as if simply writing poetry were enough to understand it, and as if poets or novelists had a right, if not a duty, to explain themselves. But there's no end to the critics' misunderstanding.) "All I did was to report . . ." they say. Or: "These are the facts. What can I do about them? . . . I was just a recording device . . . I am only guided by sincerity . . . A mirror along the road . . . the passive agent of unknown forces . . . I banished any critical thinking."

We can see where this rather suspect modesty leads. If commonplace expressions and clichés are inevitable in literature, the writer can at least proclaim his *innocence.* He is not the one who coins and imposes a cliché. He just lets it pass. It is not him saying: "The marchioness went out at five o'clock." It is the marchioness who went out. A funny idea, but it really has nothing to do with him. Neither does "the incorrigible convict and the fallen woman." No. It's his deep mind. It is something *other* within him. A little substance and a lot of art, said Racine. A little art and a lot of substance, Balzac, Stendhal, and Zola readily admitted—as did Rimbaud and Nerval too. "Your fine poem," Claudel was told. "Oh, it was nothing to do with me." Ramuz said: "I am not an artist." And Taine: "My style comes to me from the facts."

Realism and Surrealism are in the same boat here. Both encode a curious system of alibis. Put simply, in the former the writer disappears behind a human text, and in the latter behind a superhuman one.

---

4. "The writer has the right to use words he makes up himself . . . The writer expresses, he does not communicate." (Manifesto for the journal *transition,* signed by Georges Pelorson, Eugène Jolas, Camille Schuwer, etc.)

A slice of life and the slice of a dream both allow the writer to say: "I was not there." If anyone holds it against Breton for his pale angels, magic fountains, affectionate velocities, and breasts in full bloom, he says (in a somewhat solemn tone of voice): "I wrote what my thought dictated to me, independently of any aesthetic considerations." Or else: "These are the confessions of my mind; I couldn't care less about the literary consequences." Francis Jammes would say to André Gide: "I have written two bad lines of poetry here." "Then correct them." "I don't believe I have the right to." Yet at the far side of the public park stands the novelist who is so impassioned by and preoccupied with truth, facts, and observation, that he forgets he is writing. "I do not have a style," Stendhal or Zola say. "I am swept along by things themselves, and I follow them. Did I say *dreadful misfortune, receding forehead, suppressed emotion?* Well, what can I do to change them? They are facts. I'm describing a forehead that is receding, an emotion that someone is suppressing." Here the novelist, gripped by the same madness as the critic, will add: "Things are beautiful enough in their nakedness that they can dispense with veils. All your figures of style are not worth one storm, or the fear of being at sea, or a woman in tears." And again: "Forms come and go. We achieve immortality by creating living beings."[5]

So literature goes, tossed by the journalist to the psychic medium and back again. Another no less curious aspect of the illness we are concerned with is that we only agree to talk about it because it means we can hide more easily behind the thing inside us that's doing the talking. Not that I find the mystical possession or the self-effacement of critics or scholars—nor earlier in the text, the revolution—in the least bit contemptible. Far from it. I'm simply suspicious of a revolt, or a dispossession, which comes along so opportunely to get us out of trouble. I am astonished in fact to see you begin with a lie. Because you are still *writing*, whether you like it or not, and you're perfectly aware of it.

We have not lost sight of our sign. Did it seem obscure, by the way?

---

5. Emile Zola, of course.

Here is what happened, more or less (I think): a woman was walking along carrying a rose. The keeper said to her: "You know very well that no one is allowed to pick the flowers." "I had it when I came in," the woman answered. "Well, then, no one will be allowed to enter carrying flowers."

But some writers choose the strangest flowers, columbines and petunias: "Don't tell me they come from your own flower beds." Others think they can walk around with paper twists for roses. And finally there are those who protest: "Flowers in my hair? Really? Well it's nothing to do with me. I did it without thinking. I hadn't noticed they were flowers. They must have fallen out of a tree." What it really amounts to is sidestepping the need to defend oneself, rather than examining one's reasons.

It is not that these reasons are in the least bit obscure or hidden. On the contrary, there is hardly a single poet or critic who doesn't take every opportunity to mention them. They are precise. They are striking. We can readily experience them and observe them. And yet it seems to me that no one has ever taken them seriously, nor even thought about them.

The explanation for this is perhaps that they have usually seemed a little too banal, and obvious. But it is often precisely the banal which remains best hidden from us. Poetry is always showing us, in strange ways, the dog, the stone, or the ray of sun which habit concealed from us. Now suppose literary criticism also had something to reveal to us.

CHAPTER 3

❦ ❦ ❦   Words Are Frightening

The revolutionary tribunal of Arras will firstly judge
those prisoners who stand out because of their talents.
—Delegate Joseph Lebon, August 1793

There was a time when a book on "The Art of Writing" would appear
every week. Now we barely see one every twenty years. Who is in the
least bit surprised? If there is no piece of advice that does not turn
into a commonplace, nor elegant expression that does not turn into
a cliché, it is hard to imagine what teachers of style would have left to
tell us. That you need to be a daring creator, and not care about rules?
To say the opposite of what works of literature said in the past? To
forget you are writing so that you can devote yourself, heart and soul,
to the truth? All well and good. This is all typical of the kinds of fairly
short treatises that neither Maupassant nor Zola, Breton nor Aragon,
Claudel nor Ramuz have taken much beyond the limits of a decent
preface.[1] To put it simply, we have witnessed the emergence of a new
literary genre these days, which has been very successful, and which
could be called "justification" or "alibi." Its common theme would
more or less be: "The author establishes that, despite appearances, he
is not an author."

Here, too, people have felt a need to sidestep the problem. Three
critics have managed it reasonably well.

---

1. By the same token, I would also cite Curtius, E. M. Forster, or Cecchi if there was not
some value—as soon as you begin to talk about words and sentences—in remaining inside
a single language, so that this aspect of the problem at least does not vary.

The Cliché as a Sign of Inertia

Rémy de Gourmont, who avoids the problem through his detachment, studies authors in the same way that an entomologist studies caterpillars, with no hope of changing anything. Antoine Albalat, who is more naïve, assumes that attentiveness, patience, and observing great writers can turn a mediocre writer into a slightly less mediocre one. Marcel Schwob's own treatise is a simple collection of pitiful or abject phrases. These are the three most recent books on the art of style to date: *The Problem of Style, The Art of Writing,* and the *Morals of the Diurnals.*[2] What is more, they are diverse enough in their inspiration to cover the entire literary spectrum, since the first one suggests we consider as great writers Rimbaud or Mallarmé; the second, France or Loti; and the last, Jules Renard or Villiers de l'Isle-Adam.

Now although they disagree on everything else, there is one point on which Schwob, Albalat, and Gourmont are in agreement from the outset, and that is originality. The writer who counts is the one who sees with his eyes, hears with his ears, touches with his hand, feels with his whole body—and can do nothing to prevent his work betraying whatever it is about him that is unique and irreplaceable.[3] And this writer therefore takes care to steer clear of—if he has not instinctively avoided them—ready-made expressions, false elegance, and flowers. On this point, Gourmont is principally concerned with proscribing moral clichés: *a-man-who-will-stop-at-nothing, the-noble-career-of-the-military-man, the-corruption-of-evil;* Albalat proscribes picturesque clichés: *suppressed-emotions, impeccable-style, elegant-thinking.*

As for their reasons: I'll leave aside the most basic ones, which are that common sense is almost incapable of producing anything other

---

2. [The three texts are, respectively, *Le problème du style* (1902) by Gourmont, *L'Art d'écrire* (1900) by Albalat, and *Les moeurs des diurnales* (1903) by Marcel Schwob. *Trans.*]

3. Writing, Gourmont says, is "speaking a particular and unique dialect in the midst of a common language" (*La culture des idées*). Albalat's reasoning is more curious: "There is," he notes first of all, "a banal style in common usage, a clichéd style whose neutral and hackneyed expressions everyone uses. It is this style we must avoid in writing." And he adds: "Now, if there is a banal style, there must be an original style, since originality is the opposite of banality." (*L'Art d'écrire*).

than vulgar inanities. We know, since Flaubert and Bloy, that there is no "received" idea or saying in which stupidity and maliciousness are not very close to one another, in which greatness does not succumb to inanity, or martyrs to their executioners. Or that, as sensible as the idea may be, it is pointless to repeat what everyone knows, and to write volumes of which not a single line is read for the first time (and why not lines of which not a single word is read for the first time?). But more than being pointless or stupid, it seems that it is also *wrong*.

The reproach that he is being lazy or facile weighs on the writer of clichés: and Coleridge has already complained that it was easier, in this respect, to become a journalist than a cobbler.[4] Thus Albalat sees banal style as a kind of sloppiness or impotence;[5] Gourmont, as a sign of degeneration or lack of attention;[6] and Schwob, of ignorance or weakness. (And we can easily see what they mean. We generally say—almost as a cliché in itself—about someone who talks in clichés: "He didn't try very hard, he didn't go out of his way." Or else: "Watch people chatting to each other in the street . . . Their faces express nothing of the words they are saying. This is because they are not thinking, they are never thinking, they are using ready-made expressions.")[7] But we need to listen to them more closely.

"If we allow ourselves to use these ready-made expressions once," says Albalat, "we will allow ourselves to use them twice, then three times, and once we're on that slippery slope, we let ourselves go."[8] Talking of the same slope, Gourmont says: "To explain clichés all we need is the theory of association: one proverb brings another along with it; a cliché drags all of its consequences and all of its rags behind it."[9] And also: "So the stylistic form we are dealing with here is a form of verbal amnesia."[10]

We thus move imperceptibly from laziness to the reasons for this

4. *Table Talk.*
5. See especially *L'Art d'écrire*, p. 76, p. 89.
6. *Esthétique de la langue française*, p. 308 ff.
7. Paul Léautaud, *Journal*.
8. *L'Art d'écrire*, p. 76.
9. *Esthétique*, p. 309.
10. *Esthétique*, p. 308.

laziness. A commonplace expression is said to reveal a thought that is not so much indolent as it is submissive, not so much inert as it is led astray, and as if possessed. Clichés, in short, are a sign that language has suddenly overtaken a mind whose freedom and natural movement it has just constricted.

The Power of Words

"Some men," says Gourmont, "think in ready-made sentences." (Meaning a sentence is a substitute for a reflexion.) ". . . This singular ability to think in clichés . . ."[11] Or: "Words fail to arrange themselves into any new positions. They are presented in the same familiar order in which the writer's memory received them."[12] (Meaning that they drag thoughts along behind them, shamefully resigned thoughts.) And later on, when talking about writers of clichés: "These poor people, eaten up by verbalism . . ."[13] Elsewhere, Gourmont explains: "Words trapped in the brain, as if in some dispensing machine, go straight from their boxes to the tip of the lips or of the pen, without any intervening conscience or sensibility."[14]

I do not know if this explanation is right; it is at least clear, and no less banal, it must be said, than the cliché it is contesting. We can see here that critics' thinking is founded, almost formulated, upon what is without doubt the most serious reproach made in our time: that the author of commonplace expressions gives in to the power of words, to verbalism, to the influence of language, and so on. It is such a *natural* reproach that to give it a kind of presence and virtue all we have to do is to talk about "words" or "sentences"—better still, about "ready-made sentences"—in a distrustful tone of voice. And who could not in some way feel affected by it when Taine and Renan, for example, condemn half of all writers—but especially classical writers—for their "literary preconceptions." And then Proust in turn calls Renan—as Faguet does

---

11. *Esthétique,* p. 302.
12. *Esthétique,* p. 310.
13. *Esthétique,* p. 332.
14. *Le Problème du style,* p. 48.

Taine—a "cunning sentence repairman."[15] Pierre Lasserre writes of Claudel that he "abuses the most material aspects of speech."[16] Pierre Lièvre says of Moréas: "He called metaphors and noble words to arm themselves."[17] Paul Valéry likewise says of Stendhal that he "knew how to get around writing sentences *per se* . . ."[18] Charles Maurras of Victor Hugo: "It's the words themselves that rise up . . . he is no longer the one writing them."[19] And Julien Benda, about men of letters in general: "What is particular to them is that they revel in nice-sounding phrases."[20] Verlaine: "Above all, avoid style." By which we understand an *accomplished* style, a style that is just words and phrases. And who wrote the following: "Trying to represent authentic men these days is an exceptional undertaking. Just look at the books that have appeared recently: it's all just printed words derived from other printed words."?[21] But indeed who has not written, or wanted to write this sort of thing? Goethe said: "We read and write so many books that we end up turning into one." And Victor Hugo: "A poet must not write with what has already been written, but with his soul and his heart."[22] It seems, then, as if literature were bearing down with all its weight on each new writer, compelling and constricting him, so that he is only able to remain a man at the cost of an infinite flight.

This flight is so difficult, and the temptation so keenly felt, that a writer is very often viewed with suspicion before we have even studied him. Which of us has not read a new novel with these very scruples in mind? And remembering how charming we find imitation, how graceful familiar habits can seem to us, we are reassured by the awkward aspects rather than the successful ones, and vaguely disappointed if we are not disconcerted. It seems as if there were a time when books revealed man to us, or at least familiarized us with him, and took us up

---

15. Preface to *Tendres Stocks.*
16. *Les Chapelles littéraires,* I
17. *Sur Moréas.*
18. *Stendhal.*
19. *Lorsque Hugo eut les cent ans.*
20. *La jeunesse d'un clerc.*
21. Jean Prévost, *Nouvelles littéraires* (4 September 1926).
22. Préface to *Odes et Ballades.*

to his level, or even took us higher than him. Nothing today is better than an illness, a catastrophe, a love affair with an actress—in short, entertainment. Someone said to Prévost that Guenne was leaving politics in order to devote himself to art. "What a tremendous loss for art," Prévost replied.

In fact, there are a several valuable points to note about this reproach: it is clear; it is precise (whereas "taste" was really a good pretext for talking about everything and nothing, and was in fact quite arbitrary); it is presented frankly for us to observe and study. It makes for a very particular atmosphere in criticism.

Terror or, The Status of Criticism

This being, first of all, that criticism acquires a kind of natural authority that almost makes it a science, insofar as it comes *after* the work of literature. It has to wait until the literary event *has happened* before it can judge, and only then can it determine patiently whether the work of literature is repetitive or inventive, whether it is new or conventional. All true admiration is historical, said Renan. For a long time now, we have accepted that there is a kind of precautionary, creative—in a word, rhetorical—criticism, which sees its role as paving the way for plays or poems, guiding them, creating favorable conditions for them. But we begin with the poem or the play, and criticism follows, as best it can. This is what is expressed by the idea (among others) of the critic as opposed to the creator (the former being just about fit to untie the latter's shoelaces), an idea which is no less popular these days than that of the "power of words" or the "dangers of eloquence."[23]

However there is another sense in which criticism is a science, and is psychological as much as it is historical. Boileau, Voltaire, or La Harpe judged a poem according to whether it was agreeable or unpleasant, whether it conformed to or challenged good taste, rules, or

---

23. Whence one curious problem, among others: anyone wishing to give advice to a young *bourgeois* about taking up literature recommends to him that he should be an intrepid inventor, and forget what he has learned in school. But what about a peasant, or a laborer? They will be advised to forget what they have never learned.

nature. But now Schwob, Albalat, or Gourmont think we only need to "observe the mechanisms of the human mind."[24] Since Sainte-Beuve, critics have discerned a phenomenon among writers, at the very point of origin of their work, and one that inevitably brings with it credit or discredit. The evidence and symptoms of this phenomenon—of either being subjected to language or, on the other hand, freed from it—are to be found in clichés, where there is no possibility of error. It is no longer the novel which is facile, but the author who is a coward. Nor the poem which is banal or flat, but the poet who is a cheat. Nor the play which is lacking in good taste, but the playwright who is unable to think clearly. It is less the work than the writer that is being judged, and less the writer than the man. One consequence of this, among others, is the value that is given to a writer's awkwardness and to his flaws. "The work of literature," it is said, "is so well written that there is nothing left of it."[25] But one talks, conversely, about moving, delicious, or admirable flaws: because they give the author away, and reveal the man.

When there are no flaws, there is one remaining resource for critics, which is indiscretion. What they look for, turning their investigation around, is not so much even whether the writer has managed to evade the intoxicating power of words, but whether he is capable of evading it: whether his nature, his temperament, the adventures he pursues, have allowed him to resist literature. In a word, whether he is *authentic*.

Criticism thereby acquires a justifiable violence, which it never had before, since it is so much easier (and more pleasurable) to vent rage against a man than against a book. And more economical as well, since one man can be held accountable for fifty books: "One ought to punish bad writers with a firmer hand," Gourmont says. He adds: "and destroy with merciless criticism the work of imitators, smother these revolting creatures in their holes."[26]

---

24. *Esthétique*, p. 303.
25. Max Jacob, *Art poétique*.
26. *Esthétique*, p. 322. See also his *Culture des idées*, p. 4: "If there were not two kinds of literature, we would immediately have to cut the throats of every French writer." We have to take this distinction between "two kinds of literature" as a purely rhetorical formulation.

We call periods of *Terror* those moments in the history of nations (which often follow some famine), when it suddenly seems that the State requires not ingeniousness and systematic methods, nor even science and technology—no one cares about any of that—but rather an extreme purity of the soul, and the freshness of a communal innocence. Consequently citizens themselves are taken into consideration, rather than the things they do or make: The chair is forgotten in favor of the carpenter, the remedy in favor of the doctor. Skill, knowledge, and technique, however, become suspect, as if they were covering up some lack of conviction. The representative Lebon decreed, in August 1793, that the revolutionary tribunal of Arras would begin by judging those prisoners who "stood out because of their talents." When Hugo, Stendhal, or Gourmont talk about massacres and slaughters, they are also thinking about a kind of talent: the kind that is betrayed by flowers of rhetoric. As if a mediocre author—taking advantage of the effect *already* obtained by a certain arrangement of words, or a certain literary device—were happy to construct, out of bits and pieces, a machine for producing beauty, in which beauty is no less displeasing than the machine.

❦ ❦ ❦   In the monastery of Assisi, there was a monk with a thick accent which reeked of his native Calabria. The other monks made fun of him. Now he was very sensitive, and after a while would only open his mouth when announcing an accident or misfortune, that is, some event that was in and of itself serious enough for his accent to have some chance of going unnoticed. However, he liked to talk, and began to invent catastrophes. Because he was honest he went as far as causing them to happen.

And our literature likewise would not be so concerned about demanding that it be sensational, daring, and extravagant, if it did not want to make us forget that it is literature, which uses words and sentences. For this is really its secret: Its words seem dangerous, and its accent intolerable.

At least we now understand this danger in some detail, and the reasons behind this hatred.

II

The Myth of the Power of Words

CHAPTER 4

✿ ✿ ✿ Terror in More Detail

> Decadence in literature begins the day the writer,
> misled by the charms of certain phrases and, like Balzac,
> seduced by words, foolishly imagines that all he needs to
> do is to write.
> —Juvignet, *Of Decadence in Literature,* 1765

. . . for these reasons are plentiful. They would reconcile us with Terror, if it were possible. Its pretexts are certainly rather feeble: the notions of character or life are not worth a lot more than those of taste, beauty, and the other vague ideas that delighted writers at the end of the classical period. Terror is certainly both pretentious and disappointed, mad and silent. It has these faults, and many others besides. But it has one virtue that far exceeds its faults: In a field all too often caught up in its own obsessions and complacency, it categorically rejects chance, obscurity, confusion. Its apparent arguments are perhaps cowardly, but its secret proofs are admirably *precise* and urgent. If we really do need to be baroque and outlandish in order to save present-day thinking from slavery, then long live the baroque and the outlandish! If we have to suffer poverty and hunger, the same goes for poverty and hunger.

To say *precise* would not be saying much. This precision offers itself to criticism and scrutiny. Its experiment may be weak, but it is still an experiment, and it relies on us to carry it out. Its observations may be inaccurate, but they are still observations, and they rely on us to reactivate them. Precise proofs, and it is up to us to know whether they are accurate. To make them accurate, if need be. For the facts are there: clichés, grandiose words, commonplace expressions, are the easiest things there are to observe. And who would not want to treat scientifically a doctrine that presents itself to us as a science?

We need first of all examine it in more detail.

A Political Argument

Sainte-Beuve is without doubt the first critic to assign himself the task of distinguishing writers who think deeply from those who in their work surrender "to a concern for rhetoric, pure and simple." It goes without saying that the former can be more or less admirable but the latter are contemptible.

We now know how widespread this distinction has become. Sainte-Beuve only thought of condemning writers from the end of the classical period, Delille or Chênedollé. Taine suspects all works of literature written in the 18th century of being guilty of verbalism—and the writings of Jean-Jacques Rousseau in particular. For Renan, all of classical literature, with the exception of Jansenism, is compromised by its abuse of rhetoric. And for Brunetière, it is Malherbe's poetry. For Faguet, however, it is Renaissance literature that seems narrowly bound to its verbal artifices, and as if defeated by its own language. No one is safe. Lemaître berates Villon, and Gourmont Voltaire. Taine, once he is finished with Rousseau, suddenly sees Racine as the epitome of verbalism. Sainte-Beuve lets Delille go, and attacks Victor Hugo. And Marcel Schwob goes after Chateaubriand. In fact, this all seems perfectly plausible and convincing, and not without its vulgar equivalents.

For the same argument is often made elsewhere than in literature. It is common and popular. It does not so much introduce a literary or a more refined element into politics, for example, as it does a polemical element into literature. There is not one magazine or newspaper that does not invite its readers, once a week, to separate the "chaff of words" from the "wheat of things." Or that does not sigh, in talking about war or peace, about elections, about unemployment: "Words! Words! Words!" Hamlet is now a journalist.

And he's making a fortune out of it. A journal of social and political criticism has just begun a column called "The Power of Words" alongside its usual sections: "Setting the Record Straight," "Confrontations," "The Condition of the Working Class."[1] These powerful words

---

1. [This journal is *Les Nouveaux Cahiers*. This section was originally written as a "letter" to the *Nouveaux Cahiers*, first published in 1938. For the full text of this version, which

are, for example, *ideological warfare, renegade, youth, Popular Opinion, Democracy,* and other similar abstract terms. The curious implication is that such words lend themselves just as easily to observation or to criticism as the salary of a metalworker, or rent prices. What is more, it is generally accepted that analyzing them, and bringing them back to a concrete level by forcing them, in a sense, to confess their true meaning, will deprive them of their randomness, and their magical power, which is more akin to wizards' spells than to any scholarly rules.

But *Les Nouveaux Cahiers* did not discover the power of words. Quite the opposite, in fact, since there has over the last hundred years or so been no more common argument among political writers. Among *all* political writers, this argument is so valuable that it is used equally by the reactionary against the democrat as by the revolutionary against the moderate.

Thus Charles Maurras, and before him Bonald, observed that when things go wrong in society, it is not because of man's stupidity but because of language's influence. "The first reform," he says, "is to put an end forthwith to the reign of words."[2] Which words? He immediately goes on to explain: "The words *freedom, democracy,* and *equality* are eminently liable to muddle our thinking." Yet Jean-Richard Bloch, echoing Proudhon, says for his part: "Our political problems come from the power of words . . . there are large corpses lying across our path. These are dead words."[3] Which ones? He adds: "Words like *religion, order,* and *army* affect and control us as if they had retained their original meaning." When de Rougemont, Bost, or Reinach denounce the words *violence, security,* or *classes,* it is in the same tone of voice that we have heard our heads of State these days attacking the "harmful power of these empty terms *Cubism* and *Futurism*," or the expression "*equal rights,*" or "that hollow phrase, *Society of Nations.*" And so on, from one end of the spectrum to the other. Even the images and (if I

---

also informs the later section on the "The Myth of the Power of Words," see the appendix to the 1990 Folio edition of *Les Fleurs de Tarbes,* edited by Jean-Claude Zylberstein, 225–37. Trans.]

2. *Dictionnaire,* article on *mot* [word]

3. *Destin du siècle.*

can put it this way) the literary form of the argument are scarcely different. No sooner has Simone Weil warned us, in the *Nouveaux Cahiers,* against certain words "soaked in blood and tears" (such as *fascism*) than Colonel de la Rocque screams in *Le Petit Journal:* "Watch out for words covered in blood and pus!" (such as *bolshevism*).

Terror Finds Its Own Philosopher

I have been talking about the cruder forms of Terror. There are subtle ones too. Our inner life, if we are to believe Bergson, cannot be expressed without leaving behind everything that is most precious about it. Our mind is, at every point, oppressed by language. And every man, if he wants to get to his authentic thought, must eventually break through a crust of words that very quickly hardens again, and of which commonplace expressions, clichés, and conventions are merely the most obvious forms.

I hardly know of any other doctrine that is, on the face of it, more alien and more hostile to literature, or more liable to reduce it to a pile of quivering and neglected words. Yet writers have been the first to adopt it, with such enthusiasm and so completely, that we might well suspect them of having in a sense previously appealed for it, even formulated it in some confused way in advance. "I was born," says one of them, "at the age of eighteen, the day I read Bergson for the first time."[4] Another: "His *Essai* brought us to an awareness of man and of life."[5] But the unintentional testimonies are even more convincing.

It is curious to note how much Bergson's reflections on language—and on that fragile and constantly reworked language, literature—have *become* true. As if they were just what we had been waiting for. As if, once they came, we finally knew what we were dealing with.

Bergson writes as follows: "The novelist who rips apart the artfully woven fabric of our conventional self—woven from our intelligence, and even more so from language—reveals a fundamental absurdity

---

4. Charles Du Bos.
5. Gabriel Marcel.

beneath this apparent logic, and an infinite penetration beneath this juxtaposition of simple states of mind."

I only half recognize here Balzac, Eliot, Tolstoy, and the other novelists Bergson might have read. But the remark becomes admirably precise as soon as one thinks of Joyce or Proust.

So much for the novelist. Elsewhere Bergson talks about poets, and the particular obstacle that words put in their way, this obstacle which causes the essence of our thought to disappear forever, this "confused, infinitely mobile, inestimable, irrational, delicate, and fugitive element, which language is incapable of grasping without arresting its mobility, nor without adapting it to its own banal form."

He adds: "Underneath all of the joys and the sorrows that can just about be translated into words, [the poet] grasps something which has nothing to do with language, and that is the rhythms of living and breathing which are more intimately part of man than his most intimate feelings."

I can hardly recognize Rimbaud, Baudelaire, or Mallarmé here. (Or rather, if I do recognize some parts of their work, it doesn't account for the infinite care they take with language, their almost religious respect for the word.) But certainly Apollinaire, Fargue, and Eluard, with their secret desire to humiliate language—sometimes to renew it, but always feeling they are worth more than it. So much for the poet.

Yet Bergson sees the critic's work as nothing more than an attempt to get closer to, and replicate "just as a passer-by might join in a dance" the act whereby the poet or novelist, "immaterial, absent-minded, abandoning all preconceived forms and rejecting generalities and symbols . . . glimpses things in their original reality."

No, this is not Brunetière, nor Taine or Faguet. Nor is it quite Sainte-Beuve (despite what he might say).[6] But who does not recognize Thibaudet, for whom "the ideal for a critic is to coincide with the creative mind

---

6. I am thinking, more than the famous passage about the river, of the following: "Just as when a ship is in danger of being frozen in ice, we are constantly preoccupied with breaking the rigid circle that forms around it . . . so each of us should at every point be preoccupied with breaking in our minds the mould that is beginning to set and solidify. Let us not become set in our ways . . ." and so on (*Nouveaux Lundis,* VII, 49–50).

of the novelist"? Or indeed Charles Du Bos, forever concerned with avoiding "the unconscious need for symmetry which, by crystallizing the very fluid forms of our spiritual life, would separate the critic from the creator, in whose tracks he follows . . ." and really literary criticism as a whole, whose secret we analyzed earlier. It's as if Terror—which from the outset finds its artistic director, Sainte-Beuve; a little later, its disciples, Taine and Renan; then its scholars, its collectors, its men of the world, Faguet, Schwob, Lemaître; its grand inquisitors, Brunetière, Gourmont—had to wait until around 1900 for the metaphysician who would provide its demonstration, but at the same time aggravate and accelerate it.

Terror as a Method

Whatever the form in which Terror appears to us, it seems to come down to a few simple ideas, which can be easily summarized. First of all that certain words—maybe all words—are capable of exerting a singular power over the hearts and minds of men, *independently of their meaning.* "Big words," said Péguy, are the words we do not understand. For Georges Duhamel, they are the words whose appearance extinguishes our reflections and thoughts, for Jean-Richard Bloch the ones which bear absolutely no relation to the actual facts they should refer to. H. G. Wells commented in the same vein that the only words in a speech that move us and lead us to act are those whose meaning remains inaccessible, "as doctors, judges, and ministers are well aware," he added. Sometimes their meaning has disappeared, or faded away over time; the word however has not lost any of its value or weight. (As is the case, some politicians would say, with *classes* or *religion.*) And at other times words do not yet have any precise or coherent meaning. Perhaps they never will have one. This only increases their effectiveness, and seductiveness. This is true of *democracy,* or *infinity.*

As for the ways and means in which this power exerts itself, it seems that we need again to distinguish between two types: Sometimes it's the words which act directly upon the mind, lead it astray, unsettle it without allowing it to see clearly (thus we talk about words making you dizzy, about your head swimming, about sudden fits: "The poet who is prey to words ...").And at other times, it is conversely the mind which makes a coldly calculated decision to surrender its freshness and inspiration to language, rules, and clichés. (Thus a politician patiently entrusts his arguments to "freedom" and "justice"; a poet submits to rhyme, and a playwright to the dramatic unities). But whether or not it is spontaneous, habitual, or naïve, the power of words in any event reveals a gap, and almost a rupture, in the relationship within language between words and meanings, between signs and ideas. One of these two elements, whose union allows us to speak in an everyday sense, is vastly amplified, and as if hypostatized, while the other is reduced and abused. And there are, quite simply, men who accept abuse and slavery more easily and more happily than others.

Do we need to spell out the obvious even more explicitly? Yes, if we are intent on leaving nothing unclear or unnoticed. Let us say then (to put our minds at rest) that language is made up—as taught in grammar books, and as confirmed by dictionaries, if only in the way they are designed—of on the one hand signs which can be apprehended by the senses: that is, noises, sounds, written or tactile images. And on the other of ideas, which are connected to these signs in such a way that the sign evokes them as soon as it appears. In short, a body and a soul, matter and spirit. The latter subtle and supple, the former fixed and passive. They are so different from one another that nothing we can say about words can be said about ideas, and vice versa. Both are, however, so strangely familiar to us, so unquestionable and taken as *givens,* that we wonder whether our most general ideas about the material, and the inorganic, do not come to us from our having applied to the whole world what our inner experience tells us at every point about words; but also our ideas about the spirit, and life, from what language tells us about thoughts. The power of words would thus be precisely, in the microcosm of its expression, the material oppressing the spiritual. In the same way that a man, anticipating the violent blow that is about to strike him, already feels himself transformed into a corpse, so a thought that is subjugated to words, however hard it tries to keep up appearances, is already dead and reduced to nothing: just one thing among others that falls over when you push it, and that stays down once it has fallen over. And there are simply two points to make here. One is that Terror commonly accepts that ideas are *worth more* than words, and the spiritual worth more than the material: Between the two there is a difference in dignity no less than in nature. This is its principle of faith, or, if you prefer, its prejudice. The second is that language is essentially dangerous for thought: It is always ready to oppress it if we are not watchful enough. The simplest definition one can give of the Terrorist is that he is a *misologist*.[7]

If we had to pursue our analysis a little further, we would add here that the customary separation of sign and thing, word and idea, derives from the simplest, but also the most sensible, method of knowledge at our disposal: the one used by detectives just as much as philosophers, by car mechanics as much as by physicians. It consists, whenever one is faced with any difficulty—and God knows, language and expressions, advice, orders, and compliments, present all kinds of difficulties, which are forever threatening us, and forever being resolved—in reducing obscure events to their clear and distinct elements: in identifying the broken carburetor's role in your breakdown; or in singling out the wound, the revolver, the killer's fingerprints, whenever there is a murder; or in distinguishing the oxygen and hydrogen in water's composition; or within a sentence, firstly words (which may very well be invasive, overbearing, and may abuse their brute force), and then meanings. So we divide the difficulty into as many pieces as we need to resolve it, requiring each piece to present clear evidence, and taking nothing for granted that has not been verified: accepting finally that there is nothing in these elements that our attention, as soon as we apply it to them, is not capable of grasping and knowing. This is the first, extremely solid, foundation upon which Terror builds its war machine.

---

7. It would be easy to note other, more striking, effects of this *misology*. The main discoveries of our time are directed against a certain naïve understanding of "great words"—these great words that Gourmont proposes quite crudely to "sully." Marx and Freud, Sorel, or Gobineau (to mention just these authors) attempt first of all to establish that the man who talks about *freedom* or *equality*, of *rights*, or *love*, or even of a *wardrobe*, of a *flight*, or of a *ball*—and in this respect dreams are just another kind of language—is not *entirely* thinking what he seems to be thinking. So true is it that the most elementary reactions with regard to language govern the preoccupations of an age, and even the most disinterested research.

❦ ❦ ❦   If I try to tease out the particular *concern* which motivates Terror in literature, I find that a poem or a novel no doubt expresses joy and despair, or shows people and the way they lead their lives, but more secretly reveals an *idea about language:* the understanding we have of it; armed with this understanding, the attitude we take with respect to it; how we place ourselves in relation to it, and in *opposition* to it—people's way of living and their joy would in fact be no more than the appearance of this understanding of language, this technique bearing on language.

This is Terror's other secret. And I don't know how well-founded it is. But we must confess that in light of our first observations it is not entirely implausible. For we have at least discovered that a certain critical attitude, along with the works that are produced by it, with the revolt, the poverty, and the excess that follow from it, depends upon a very precise opinion about language.

This opinion is not without its faults—or at the very least a few obscurities.

CHAPTER 5

❧ ❧ ❧ In Which the Reader Sees the Author the Other Way Round

> As soon as there are people in the world who are experts on horses, we see a number of remarkable riders appear. The truth is that these riders have always been around, but it is the experts that are rare.
> —Han Yu, *Reflections on Horsemen*, 815

Terror has two equally notable traits. The first derives from the gravity of the question it is asking (and of the answer it is proposing). Of all the different kinds of problems posed by the practice, indeed the very existence of literature, there is one of which the others are merely reflections or signs: and every writer is judged according to the way he solves it, either openly or secretly. That is, whether literature nurtures or ruins the only event that matters: the mind and its freedom. And we also maintain that this conviction limits and predetermines just about every opinion or taste Pierre Lasserre expressed about the Romantics, Taine about writers from the 18th century, Renan the 17th century, or Faguet the 16th. Just about all of our opinions of authors are colored by a violent and quickly-formed sense of their attitude to words and sentences.

Terror's second trait is its frivolousness. It appears to make do, when dealing with such a serious matter, with first impressions.

We Ask Scholars, but to No Avail

According to the Terrorist, all he is doing is stating a fact, and something like a linguistic law: namely that certain words reveal a hypertrophy of matter and of language, at the expense of ideas. Now, there is not a single linguist who seems to have noticed this law of expression. Not a single grammarian. Not a single philologist. I cannot see any of them, from Meillet to Nyrop, from Hermann Paul to Bally, who has pointed out this singular influence that politicians and moralists are always droning on about. This in itself is not surprising. In fact they have pointed out exactly the opposite.

For there are two semantic laws on which they all more or less agree. The first one has to do with the *wearing away of the senses*. It contends that words gets worn out before ideas, and their expressive value easily fades or disappears altogether, and does so the more striking and alive the idea is. It has reached the point where the linguistic awareness of a people has to be put to work, unconsciously but obstinately, either by maintaining the value of the terms it uses, or by substituting new terms which can do the same job. When *garce* deviated from its meaning, our linguistic awareness invented *fille* [*girl*]; and *jeune fille* [*young girl*], when *fille* in its turn took on other meanings.[1] Far from being the case that words survive ideas, it is ideas that survive words.

The second law has to do with this linguistic awareness. It contends that common sense, when dealing with language, has an unerring instinct; that it accurately perceives the most minute variations in meaning, well before grammarians and linguists; that it can teach writers themselves, and that in Les Halles people do not only learn to speak, they learn to *hear*. In short, no one has ever seen a word act according to a meaning it does not have.

All of this leaves little room for the power of language. The fact remains that the event in question is too subtle or secret to be subjected to scholarly analysis. (And I can think of nothing more elusive than how a word influences the flow of our ideas.) Bergson points out in this regard that language and thought are contrary in nature: the latter is fugitive, personal, unique; the former is fixed, shared, abstract. Consequently thought, which in any case has to go through the language that expresses it, is thereby altered, and becomes in its turn, because

---

1. [*Garce* is nowadays more or less equivalent in meaning and pejorative force to "bitch," but it was originally the feminine form of *garçon*, boy. *Fille* is now used pejoratively for *fille de joie*, prostitute. *Trans.*]

of this constriction, impersonal, inert and drained of all its color. Now (Bergson adds), this kind of thought lends itself better to the demands of society than the other kind, replacing it little by little, and leading us further and further away from ourselves. The facts are plainly there for us to see: Which of us has not felt thwarted in advance and as if deformed by the words we are about to say?

Here again, though, we run into more obstacles: first of all, that it is unwise to reduce all language to *expressing* thoughts. Phèdre speaks, on the contrary, in order to play a role, and to hide her feelings; and Ariste speaks for the sake of speaking, saying anything that comes into his head. So their thought, concealed behind words, is quite free to follow the wildest of reveries.

But even if I grant that all language expresses something, I do not in the least consider that this expression must necessarily diminish me. Quite the opposite, in fact: All it takes is a few words that a book or some other man tells me, for me to be thrown into an extraordinary and unexpected inner life. A few words? It sometimes only takes a single word that I have just uttered. Our language, said Comte, teaches us about ourselves, or as Rilke put it, reveals us to ourselves.

But supposing I want all language to express something, and all expression to constrict us. It would still have to be proven that this constriction is permanent. Here again I can see quite the opposite, that *once a word has been spoken,* it can leave my inner life in complete disorder, and that I can feel all the more free because I was so constricted. As soon as I find myself caught between this inexpressible mixture of love and hatred, of gratitude and contempt, it takes revenge on me because of the contrived simplicity that my words forced upon it. The survivor of a shipwreck waving a cloth rag on his raft communicates his hunger, his thirst, and his worry very poorly. Before speaking of the strange simplifying effect that the rag has on him, I would really like to be sure that his worry, his hunger, and his thirst will not return as soon as the ship has passed him by. The facts, Bergson and the Terrorists say, are there for all to see. That may well be. But the opposite facts are no less there for all to see. Let us get back to our writers.

How Frivolous the Critics' Way of Thinking Is

If there is one aspect of the literary judgments we have been looking at that is likely to surprise us, it is that critics hardly ever think to
justify them. It is as if they were so obvious as to be self-evident, and
as if we only needed to say them for them to be right. Faguet stops at
the impression that Montaigne's "ruses" and "devices" make upon
him—but the real question is knowing whether Montaigne *thinks* of
them as ruses and devices. Brunetière and Renan state that Malherbe
and other classical writers pride themselves on obeying the rules of
rhetoric; they forget to enquire whether rhetoric is for these writers
simply an art of speaking and writing, or whether it is an art of thinking. Taine becomes indignant when he sees Jean-Jacques laboring over
his style—but what if Jean-Jacques only wanted to better mold his style
to his thinking? Sainte-Beuve reproached Romantic writers for being
a little bit too *preoccupied* with the genres and rules they were trying
to destroy. But he does not think about proving the only point worth
proving: that is, whether Romantic writers are attached to these genres
as genres—and not to their own emotion and freedom, insofar as they
think they are escaping these genres. So, for example, I might assume
that the author of a "well-written" text was only thinking about grammar and rules. But I might just as well assume that the nature and the
exercise of these rules had made them so habitual that he is finally as
free as anyone can be to forget about them. Who is more keenly concerned about corrections and rules when he has to write something:
an uneducated or an educated person? It is something we must at least
consider. It is not saying much in these cases to claim that Terrorists
do not provide any proof; they do not even seem to think, and this is
the most serious point, that they ought to provide any.

I accept that proof is no easy task. The only way we are normally informed about the relationship between a writer and his work is through
the work itself as it yields to our imagination: Should we wish to take
it as a collection of artistically assembled words and sentences, this is
what it immediately becomes. Should we only wish to retain the meaning and the emotion it contains, then it empties itself of language to

become nothing but thought. We can thus, with equal ease, either give in to its style or its inspiration. This does not imply we can't admit that the writer wrote it in the same order in which we think it; but this is precisely not to reflect upon it, or to be in possession of any valid proof. What remains to be done is for us to obtain a few confessions from the authors themselves.

What they confess is the exact opposite.

Charles Maurras, Jules Lemaître, and André Gide all agree in acknowledging that the Romantics were the first French writers to have made language take clear precedence over feeling, and words over thoughts. Yet the Romantics, using the same evidence, consider themselves the first writers to have completely freed thought from the constraints of words. Victor Hugo is without doubt the poet critics are least reluctant to talk about every now and then (with regret) in terms of empty verbalism; but he is certainly the first poet to have seen himself as the personal enemy of empty verbalism. Gourmont writes of Chateaubriand that he is the "victim of his style." But no writer has believed himself more sincerely to be the victim of his stormy emotions. If there is one aspect of Stendhal that never fails to irritate us, it is, according to Valéry, "the natural tone he affects," and the means by which he "accumulates in each of his works all of the most eloquent symptoms of sincerity." But who wanted more passionately than Stendhal to free himself from tone and literary artifice? And Faguet, finally, can write of Taine that his language is "completely artificial," that it only achieves any depth "by a miracle of fabrication." But Taine says (and who would question the word of this honorable man?): "All I am doing is describing how I feel . . . My style comes from the facts I am dealing with."

And so it goes for the diverse schools which have followed on from Romanticism. Whether it is Symbolism or Unanimism, the Paroxysts or the Surrealists, with each and every one of them we cannot fail to be struck these days by their verbal idiosyncrasies. Furthermore, every one of them has believed it was based on a rejection of verbalism and literary artifice—and each and every one of them begins by discovering, with abundant energy, a particular object (the mind, man, society, the unconscious) which, it seems to them, the previous schools took it upon themselves to hide behind words.

I am not trying to judge writers or critics. I am only surprised by a misunderstanding between them that seems quite consistent, and as if determined by a law. I am even more astonished by a doctrine that takes such a misunderstanding as its foundation and the heart of its meaning.

A Singular Confusion

So scholars, who should be best able to see it, never notice anything in language that resembles the power of words. But critics, who think they see it all the time, are only able to on the condition that they ignore the basic precautions that a scrupulous observer takes in similar circumstances. I do not wish to cast doubt on the existence of this power. Yet it must be a strange kind of power if, in order to see it, you have to cover your eyes.

We might have made this point to begin with: If there is one particular feature in the observations we have been looking at, it is that not one of them can offer us any *direct* testimony. Agreed, it would be rather odd for Monsieur Charles Maurras to come and say to us: "This is the effect that the word *tradition* has on me"; or for Monsieur Jean-Richard Bloch to say: "This is how the word *revolution* affects me, and guides my thinking." Of course not. They only ever talk about other writers.

More than this, though, they talk about other writers *when they are wrong,* and we can clearly identify where they go wrong: They are as different from us as they could possibly be—adversaries, enemies. H. G. Wells pointed out the danger of using ready-made words in literary criticism, because of the fixed nuances of praise or blame they carry (as is the case, for example, with a *serialized novel* or a *theatre of ideas*). He adds: "Because they are widely used by imbeciles." Granted. It goes without saying that Wells is not an imbecile; and that the Heads of State we were talking about are fortunately exempt from the intellectual decadence (as they say) displayed in mindlessly repeating such phrases such as *cubism, equality of rights, Society of Nations;* or that Monsieur Maurras is not in the least bit fooled by the word *religion,* nor Monsieur Jean-Richard Bloch by the word *democracy.*

That may well be the case. But please stop talking to me about an intimate and subtle event. If it were intimate, you would not see it. For you, Jean-Richard Bloch, are not religious, nor are you, Maurras, a democrat. Quite the opposite, in fact, and if I really wanted to know what goes on secretly in the mind of a democrat or a believer, I would not come to you to ask for advice.

We need to be more emphatic. The power of words, far from ever yielding to the laws of methodical observation in cases like this, seems to surface in every case in which this observation remains incomplete or impossible, and it seems that this failure of observation might, in some mysterious way, be a function of this power. "Julien Benda," writes one polemicist, "talks with the most fervent conviction about what is True, and Just, and Good. For him these words possess every virtue and deservedly carry with them every conviction . . ."[2] That may be true, but for Julien Benda the good and the just are, on the contrary, the very principle and truth by dint of which everything else appears as mere words and phrases: "Do you mean to say," the Christian asks the atheist, "that all I have to do in order to convince you is to mention the words Humanity, Nature, and Evolution? Can you really call it thinking if you subject yourself to these empty expressions?" But the atheist replies: "I know of no other reality that could be more universal, or further from an empty expression than Nature and Evolution." "The word *Liberty,*" said Novalis, "has produced millions of revolutionaries." No doubt: All those for whom Liberty was the opposite of a word.

We could get a little closer to the error, or difference. We are always talking about a writer's characteristic "language," the terms he is fond of, the expressions he invests—and which invest him—with a particular meaning: about his *key words.* These are Hugo's *infinite depths,* Gautier's *essential-oil burners;* the Symbolists' *torches of love, funeral urns of memory,* and *hourglasses of time.* The same could also be said

---

2. H. Plisnier, *Le Monde,* 7 May 1929.

of Valéry's *pure,* Gide's *gratuitous,* Bergson's *intuition,* or Maurras's *swarm.* That's all very well. However, anyone who makes the effort of shifting suddenly from the outside to the inside, and going from the state of being a reader to that of being an author, will no doubt feel that *swarm, gratuitous,* and *intuition*—far from being clever and useful words—are on the contrary the truth, or the *central* thought expressed or served by more common ideas and words in Bergson, Gide, or Maurras. The illusion is thus done away with. The abbé de Saint-Pierre thought a great deal about the vanity of human judgment. He reached the point where he would say, every time he approved of something: "This is good, for me, for right now." This saying took on a proverbial quality. But when someone joked with him one day about his expression, he exclaimed: "An expression, you imbecile! This is a truth it has taken me thirty years to discover."

We should define more precisely the illusion that seems to be operating here, and so inevitably that even the subtlest or most carefully worded remark is unable to avoid it. "When I eat a dish that is supposedly exquisite," writes Bergson, "the name it bears, magnified by the universal approval bestowed upon it, comes between my physical sensation and my awareness of the dish itself; I may think that it is the taste I like, whereas a slight effort of attention would prove the opposite." But I find it hard to see anything more here than a play on words. If I say that an ortolan tastes good, my approval is directed at the *bird itself,* which is called an ortolan. If, on the other hand, I approve of the *word* ortolan, I may find it graceful or sweet-sounding, but I have no desire to eat it.

❦ ❦ ❦   I certainly don't hold it against our critics for asking the essential question from the outset. What else but the essential could we be interested in, unless we're simply to be imbeciles? But I do have to reproach our critics for addressing this essential question without due caution or sufficient evidence, for talking about it so lightly and, I fear, for coercing me into hasty support by taking advantage of the state of impatience and concern its presence throws me into; who would not rush to the aid of a thought that was being mistreated?

Yet has anyone stopped to consider whether it is *actually* being mistreated? There are crimes that are so heinous that people immediately become suspicious of you merely for talking about the guilt of the person accused—as if the horror that the crime necessarily evokes ought to resist all analysis, and as if you are suspected of being immoral for having remained open-minded. The same is true of the opinion I have been looking at. It is certainly weak and unproven, and randomly condemns thousands of innocent victims. This is because it uses a kind of blackmail in order to impose itself on us. It's as if we were complicit with it, and it reminded us in conspiratorial tones about some corpse between us. We surrender to it before it has presented its evidence.

We would certainly feel uneasy about surrendering to it later on.

CHAPTER 6

❦ ❦ ❦   Terror Is Seen to Be Wanting

> I saw clearly that he was mistaken, but without being
> able to tell if it was because he was too intelligent or too
> stupid. And that he was acting badly, but without being
> able to tell if it was out of excessive goodness, or excessive
> treachery.
>
> —Mme de Graffigny, *Elisa,* III

It is not hard to understand the reason for our uneasiness: and it might
appear more serious than Terror as a whole. Bergson writes that he
proposes nothing that observation and experience have not rigorously demonstrated to him. That may be true. But nothing either for
which a more sustained observation, and *repeated* experience, have
not demonstrated the exact opposite. All we have to do is to question
the author after the reader, and (if I may say so) the *speaker* after the
person spoken to.[1]

But there is doubtless a way of avoiding this confusion. This is—ig-
noring the popular use of argumentation, and the appeal it makes to
all sorts of vague opinions—to go back to our Terror. If expressions
as clear and distinct as commonplaces and poetic phrases are a sign of
language encroaching upon the mind, then this fact ought to be easy
to understand, if indeed it is exact—or, if it is inexact, it ought to be
easy to explain.

---

1. In truth it is completely different to address someone in order to entertain or inform
them, than to order them or to influence them, in a word, to act upon them. This could
be quite well conveyed by the difference between a transitive *speaking* and an intransitive
speaking.

In Which the Author Invents His Commonplace Expressions

Paul Bourget writes: "Even though he had only ever led the *very frivolous life of a man-about-town,* in the air of the lagoon he had *savored the taste of beautiful things . . . Falling under the spell* of these paintings' *charms,* he went into raptures about such a *profusion of masterpieces.* The *mysterious languor . . .*"

Francis Carco: "*Habit governed* her every gesture . . . a bitter, delightful sensation *rose up from deep within her . . .*" And Pierre Decourcelle: "*The village clock struck midnight* when our hero . . ." Here, then, are a few commonplace expressions. I've chosen ones that are as varied as possible, and diverse in value (but nothing must seem as strange right now as "literary value")—ones that are very clear, in fact, and which make immediate sense, such that it shouldn't be difficult to discover how they were written, and how they were thought.

I must at this point make one initial comment. However banal a commonplace expression may be, it is always possible that it was invented by the person uttering it; if this is the case, it is even accompanied by a strong feeling of newness. Who would not feel humiliated, when leafing through the *Dictionary of Received Ideas* or some other collection of clichés, to find in it the very "thought" (and the word already tells us a lot) we believed we had invented; the very sentence we had up until then been saying quite innocently? Every one of us has had occasion to observe: "If you saw that sunset in a painting, you would say it was unreal." Or even: "Bronze will always hold its value." Not without a certain self-satisfied complacency. Likewise, the same tales, the same sayings, seem to originate simultaneously in countries that are very far apart, and to keep reappearing indefinitely—but not necessarily without any effort or joy in imagining them. A poet observes that the sky is starry, says so quite innocently, and takes pleasure in saying so. Why could Bourget not have invented, by himself, *mysterious-languor,* and Carco, all on his own, the *habit-which-governs?* There once lived an illiterate and slightly wild butcher boy in Rennes who around 1897, after fifteen years of obscure research, discovered how blood circulates. Now we could feel sorry for him that he had never thought of opening, or have someone read to him, a treatise on physiology. But the last thing we would reproach him for would be to accuse him of laziness or inertia. Likewise, the novelist who is *happy* to write "the clock struck midnight . . ." perhaps displays a certain freshness of sensibility, a certain naivety of imagination. He sees this night, he hears the clock strike, and he is delighted. He expects the reader to be as delighted as he is (and he is not always wrong). Poetry is also seeing with fresh eyes what everyone always sees.

Could we say that the butcher was ignorant, whereas Carco or Decourcelle are not? But there's a world of difference between physiology and literature, and the truth of an event, the urgency of a reflection, are enough to make us forget the phrases we formerly used to talk about them. Or at least to make it seem to us as if they were no longer phrases. The following dialogue conveys just this: "I am duty bound to . . ." "Duty is just a word." "Yes, when you use it,"[2] where the clear implication is: *You* may well only have in mind words and phrases when you talk about duty. But for me it's the complete opposite. And this one as well: "If I say that the morning is radiant, and that the clock struck midnight, it is true that I find myself talking like a book. But I didn't say these things *in order* to talk like a book. I said them because they are true."

To which we should add that commonplace expressions usually originate in some felicitous or surprising remark—otherwise how would they be so successful? *Mysterious-languor, melting-eyes,* and even *the-heart-of-the-gathering* [*le-sein-des-assemblées*] are not without a certain charm for anyone who hears them with an innocent ear. The writer who reinvents them feels that same pleasure: He has never felt freer, or more open to the spirit itself of the words. And what young author these days does not feel violently personal, *definitively* personal, at the very moment he invents (along with all the other young authors) a commonplace expression whose eloquence he has to wring by the neck?

---

2. Henry Bordeaux, *Les Roquevillard.*

In Which the Author Uses a Cliché

But let us suppose that invention played no part, that Bourget, Carco, and Decourcelle in fact used commonplace expressions *as such*. What does this mean, except that the expression has for them become ordinary and faded, that it has lost its picturesque quality and its detail? It is true that we no longer notice the *joie* [joy] in *feu-de-joie* [firework]; nor the *sein* [breast] in *sein-des-assemblées* [in the heart of the gathering]. We say that a *fille-de-joie* [prostitute] cries, and that a *feu-de-joie* was pathetic, without any malicious intention, and with no more awkwardness than we would feel in noting that a *belette*[3] [weasel] is ugly, a *nécessaire de toilette* [toiletries case] is unnecessary, and a *commode* [chest of drawers] is incommodious. But these phrases become just like single words that we use—and the more widely used they are, the more they are just like all other words. Thus mysterious-languor becomes a variety of languor, the fiery brunette [*brune-piquante*] just another type of brunette, and the habit-which-governs, one of a thousand effects habit can have on us (alongside habits which insinuate, those that blind, and so on).[4]

This may well be true. Only it seems that in this case the use of a commonplace expression poses no *particular* problem. If a cliché suffers from being used as a word—like any other word—it is because a thought can pass through it with no greater difficulty than it would feel in using words like *accoutumance* [familiarization], *parti pris* [bias], or *dégoût* [disgust], whose origin and etymology are no less clear. I don't see any verbalism here.

On the contrary, we could say that commonplaces are, in a sense, the place where we see a constant, obstinate attempt to create words. Linguists have occasionally searched (without success) for the origin of language. But there is one kind of language which, at every moment, originates before our very eyes—or at least tries to do so. All families, all clans, all schools, make up their own "words" and familiar expres-

---

3. *Belette* could be read as *belle-ette* (little pretty one).
4. "A figure which has become a commonplace," according to Nodier, "is nothing but the cold equivalent of the word in its literal sense." (*Dictionnaire des onomatopées*)

sions, which they invest with a secret meaning that is hidden from outsiders. The same is true, in wider communities, of slang, in-jokes, and sayings: Innumerable new terms that come into being take on different connotations, then have a single meaning, and finally disappear—covering in the space of a few years, sometimes a few days, the entire lifespan of a commonplace expression. Now, if there is one thing about our everyday experience, it is that when we use terms such as these, they do not give us the slightest impression (even if they happen to give this impression to our neighbors) of verbalism. Our thought never seems more freed from language to us than when we use them. It is as if the very effort we make in helping to give them a meaning that differs from their apparent meaning—and, if you like, the event of expression itself—compelled us to forget later on everything that is not related to this meaning; or quite simply as if a word that derived its meaning from our goodwill seemed naturally richer in memories and allusions than one whose meaning comes from a dictionary. (It may be that a sense of pride in one's *personal* language helps this feeling along). I happily accept that sayings give anyone who hears them uncharitably the impression of a phrase that is repeated at random. But, conversely, the person uttering them discovers with joy the many thousands of ingenious applications that the expressions "Do you realize," "Goodbye and thank you," and "All you have to do is . . ." lend themselves to with the same sense of happiness. And we all know, too, that the most innocent and sincere souls, who could not care less about words, often pour out their feelings in proverbs, banal sayings, and commonplace expressions. Love letters are a good example of this: infinitely rich and exceptionally meaningful for the person writing or receiving them—but puzzling to an outsider because of their banality and (he will say) their verbalism.[5]

What we have discovered is not unrelated to what we were looking for: It is exactly the opposite. Critics began by warning us that a writer of clichés found himself in a singular position with respect to

---

5. In the same way, a writer who rereads the things he wrote when he was young is constantly struck by how artificial and wordy they are. But when he was writing them, it was on the contrary their spontaneity and their effusiveness which delighted him.

language—and we discovered that he was indeed in a singular position. Our observation, and theirs too, is centered on one and the same fact: that a given phrase can be marked by a kind of hypertrophy of language and of words. Only what we discovered, at the place indicated, was a strange absence of language and almost a hypertrophy of thought.

So that the observation upon which Bergson and the Terrorists founded their doctrine appears to us, *in every case,* to be illusory and false. The most curious thing is that it is equally false for these two opposing reasons: either because the cliché is reinvented—so that the author is attached to its truth more than to its words. Or because it is simply repeated and habitual—and this habit means that the words go unnoticed. In fact, this singular kind of sentence seems to be designed to contradict everything we can imagine saying about it—as if critics talked of verbalism only in relation to those sentences which make us completely *forget* they are sentences and words, those most likely to give us a feeling of purity and innocence.

This excess of error gives us pause for thought.

The Power of Words, the Siren, and the Minotaur

Instead of clichés, we could just as well have looked at genres, dramatic unities, versification, rhyme, and the other literary conventions which Terror accuses, no less than it does commonplace expressions, of favoring language over thought. We would have thus been led, along the same lines, to note that these different conventions (however common they may be) are sometimes the object of invention or reinvention—and the author's mind is completely captivated, and delighted, by their charm and by the particular effect of their meaning. But at other times they seem to be composed according to rules—and so are automatic, rendered so transparent and invisible by overuse that they simply let through the events and passions they are responsible for expressing. A detached spectator can see a chess game as a combination of abstract rules, and the family home as a kind of prison. But a chess player feels as free and powerful as a great captain, and the father of the family is the only man in the world who can play at being a horse whenever he likes. We noted that Terrorists do not hesitate, if need be, to criticize games and families. But if they are in agreement—and us along with them—about attacking clichés with a particular ferocity, we suspect we know the reason why; it is not that clichés are in any way exceptional, since just like rhythm, rhyme, genre (and the family) they are made up of a given material element to which certain thoughts correspond. It is simply that, being shorter, they are a thousand times easier to present, manipulate—and judge—than a play or a lyric poem, and, of course, than a family. So that out of a large number of equally odious characters, we often end up most hating the one that fate has placed directly in front of us.

In fact our discovery has cleared up more than one mystery, which was holding us up a short while ago.

If Charis starts to cry when someone says to her "Your father is dead," I won't go around saying that the word *father* or the word *dead* have a strange power over her. If Denis learns that he has won a million francs and faints with joy, I won't be astonished at the state he has been thrown into by the word *million*. I know very well that it is the event, not the word, which affects them. But what about *justice,* what about *democracy* or *freedom*? For those who jump for joy at these words, it is certainly the thing itself that moves them. Even if this thing still remains variable and badly-defined when there are several different people talking together. As is the case with a commonplace expression (but on a much larger and more diverse scale), I never know exactly *which* freedom, or justice, Denis or Jacques are so enthralled by. We are always, in short, dealing with an abstract term whose applications are infinitely varied. And one could say that Terrorists, too, talk almost indiscriminately of a power of abstraction, of a power of words. Smith remarked one day on the power that words ending in -*tion* have: cooperation, temporization, constitution. When he thought he could pronounce *inundation* with the same gravitas, he did not have the success he expected. Having so much faith in the influence of a word, of a syllable, threatens here to lead us astray. In fact, there is a sort of violent absurdity in wanting to imagine such a power. For the simplest experiment teaches us that whenever there is power, words seem to be invisible; and when words do appear, there is no longer any power. It has been said that nobody is aware of the power words have on them. No doubt. But anyone can see when it has happened to them in the past. Then the error is that much more striking and plain to see. "I let myself be taken in," says one young woman, "by his beautiful, empty phrases." Well it's because what she saw was not empty phrases, but true love. "God, duty, the things they made me swallow," says a worker, "with their grandiose words." It was because he saw in them not words, but grandiose truths. But (the Terrorist will say) it's the word, or the sentence, which appear to him now, isn't it? True enough. But now that he has been disillusioned, God too has ceased to have the slightest power over him. Like sirens or the minotaur, the power-of-words is formed, through a strange kind of telescoping or joining together of two foreign and irreconcilable bodies.

I am not saying that this power of words is for all that unnecessary. It concerns us, and makes us want to talk. It may also be useful to us in other ways.

More than one child has happened to imagine some day, with the most profound feeling of joy, that he has invented thought, and that he is the only person to have ever invented it, whereas everyone else (and especially grown-ups) is only putting words together. I don't suppose there is a more delightful or thrilling impression in the world than this one, nor one that helps us to think better. There are men who have remained children on this point—who knows, they are no doubt the same ones who talk so readily about the power of words. But we have moved on from them.

✸ ✸ ✸   It is fashionable these days to be against refuting things. People say we are just being negative, or too simple in our criticism. As if it went without saying that we are naturally empty, deprived of faith and of ideas, and that science or philosophy alone should provide them for us.

Yet what if it were the other way round? What if we were in fact filled with illusory ideas and false beliefs, which stifled the truth within us? The most urgent and creative task of our mind would then no doubt consist in ridding us of such obstacles and illusions, and freeing up the space for true knowledge.

This is how Terror sees it at any rate. Gide, Valéry, and Maurras are astonished at the wastefulness of the systems, poetic methods, and barely comprehended principles which seem to them to define the times. That's the least of it! What if the very thought, which we trust to guarantee a relationship with our mind, stated that as soon as systems and poetic methods, principles and poems, take shape, as soon as they are given linguistic form, they lose their essence and their value for us? But this kind of thinking is false, and an entire world is joyfully presented to us!

Let us not neglect to give this world back to Gourmont, to Alerte, to the man rendered speechless. All I wanted to do was to protect them from themselves.

III

Inventing a Rhetoric

CHAPTER 7

❦ ❦ ❦   An Optical Illusion

> When he was seven, Harry wanted to be a girl. He was
> reaching the age when children fall in love: Finding the
> company of girls extremely charming, he imagined that
> he would feel this charm even more keenly if he himself
> were a girl.[1]
>
> —R. Hughes, *A High Wind in Jamaica*

We had to admit that Terror has one particular merit: It relies solely on observation and experience, without ever asking us to surrender meekly to feelings, or to the taste for surprise or mystery. It is, in short, perfectly scientific and wise (despite appearances to the contrary) and worthy of an age—our own—in which nothing is certain, except for one clear idea. Only this idea makes our discovery all the more disconcerting.

For Terror, when it was put to the test, was found to have been mistaken in what it observed. Its experiment was false, and its conclusion fanciful. What science shows us is the exact opposite of what we were told. We have, then, come up against the strangest of obstacles.

I am by no means saying that we should abandon our method. But perhaps we should vary and refine it somewhat.

We only have to read a poem, a speech, or the text of an advertise-

---

1. [Richard Hughes, *A High Wind in Jamaica* (London: Chatto and Windus, 1929). Paulhan's quotation here is from a French translation of the novel, which he appears to have altered. The passage from the original English text reads as follows: "Harry did not confide it to Edward, but he also, *now*, wished he was a girl. It was not for the same reason: younger than Edward, he was still at the amorous age; and because he found the company of girls almost magically pleasing, fondly imagined it would be even more so if he were one himself" (148–49). *Trans.*]

ment, to listen to a political debate or a domestic quarrel, to notice that even the most trivial of our activities involves many more arguments and reasons than we are capable of grasping, or even of *understanding*. Getting to the bottom of them is beyond us. Anyone who tries to recall them and express them using clear ideas only does so by thoroughly distorting them—as a result, their virtue and true meaning gets lost. But one might hope that a *refined* method would allow us to push things a little further, and resolve the problems raised by this initial refutation.

The Reader Finds He Is Involved

It is not without a certain sense of pleasure that we discover a commonly held opinion to be wrong. But if it is so *absolutely* wrong that all anyone needs to do to understand the error is to refer to the simplest experience, a more curious problem arises, and perhaps a more difficult one, which is why it ever became an opinion: How it could have been formed, and from what? Why was it useful, and in what ways? In short, the question is no longer whether it is true or false, but how it could *be* at all.

There is one point at least that we are tempted to concede to Terror, and that is the violence, as well as the justice, of the concern motivating it when it maintains that man must not be *too* preoccupied with language. It is true, and we cannot stress this enough, that the attention we pay to words *as such,* if it goes on for too long, can be dangerous: At the very least it creates a delay, and a kind of short-circuiting, of meaning. The law governing common expression means that words disappear fairly quickly as soon as the thing is mentioned. And nobody would disagree with the Terrorists that it is undignified for the mind to prowl around a word like an animal that is tied up; for it to remain at the stage when it first learns to talk; for it to be more worried about commas, rules, and unities than about *what* it needs to say; for it to be endlessly weighing up and comparing words, without ever moving on to things. In fact, who would not agree with them, spontaneously and enthusiastically? (But, as we saw, this is where the strength of the argument comes from—as if Terror were banking on the state of anxiety we are thrown into at the mere suspicion of an unworthy or diminished thought, in order to get us to surrender immediately to the myth it is proposing.)

And yet anybody who now wishes to pay attention not so much to this myth, as to the reasoning behind it which we have denounced, notices something curious.

If there is anything despicable or cowardly about thinking *around* a word, and thereby subjecting one's thought to language, you don't have to look very far to find the guilty party: We are the ones who have just been caught out. If we have to consider that a mind which is happy to circle around and around a sentence, without ever moving beyond it to things themselves, is a disagreeable and unworthy mind, then these are precisely the feelings that the preceding pages may have aroused. And what have we been doing if not doggedly pursuing and weighing up—without ever *settling* on any one of them—the different meanings that one and the same expression or saying or commonplace can have, depending on whether it is used often, or is new, is invented, or said mechanically? We have not been talking about languor or charm for almost a hundred pages, but only about the words that refer to charm or languor. It may well be that clichés cause anyone using them to stop worrying, more than would normally be the case, about words and sentences, but they have reminded us, more than would normally be the case, of this very same worry. It may well be that clichés reveal an author to be freer from verbalism than we would like, but they have subjected us to this verbalism, more than we would like. We have ourselves become the thing we were pursuing. We are ourselves at stake.

Hawthorne tells the story of a novelist who one day sees his characters escaping him. His hero (whom he was imprudent enough to depict as himself) rushes headlong into a catastrophe—from which he suddenly realized he himself would not, alas, escape. This is more or less our story. And it is no longer Bourget or Carco whose thought must now seem as if it is enslaved to words and sentences—but ourselves, and our own thought *when we read Bourget's and Carco's commonplace expressions.*

Now it is not that we have been, or tried to be, an exceptional reader. No, just a little bit more diligent, or more pedestrian. Our comments are the same as those that would occur to anyone in similar circumstances. And not only in books:

"What?" a father says to his son, "So you think duty is nothing but a word? You're the kind of person who doesn't care about anything, you don't believe in God or the Devil . . ." But the son thinks to himself, all flustered: "What on earth is he on about? Does he think I'm really like that? Does he think he's just making it up? Or that he can get rid of a chore just like that, without thinking?" A lover likewise says: "It's as if I've known you for ever. In what country, long ago . . .?" and a politician: "The rising tide of democracy obliges us to . . ." To which the undecided elector, or the object of the lover's affection, replies: "What is he after? Does he believe what he's saying? Or is he just trotting it out without thinking? If he imagines he's going to convince me with his grandiose words . . ."

"His grandiose words . . ." Here we come back to our reproach. It has the humblest of origins. There is no lover or ungrateful son who does not use the same reasoning as the Terrorists. Yet the illusion is all the more obvious.

The Illusion of Projection

All it takes is a few words to denounce this illusion: It is not the author, but the *reader* of commonplace expressions who finds himself all preoccupied with words and sentences. And it is easy to see why, because the author—whatever the particular meaning of the terms *freedom,* or *frivolous existence,* that he has chosen—embraces this meaning, and in the same rush of enthusiasm with which he has chosen it, finds himself fully within his mind, and given over exclusively to thought. But what else can the reader do, caught between two *equally* possible meanings, hesitating and feeling his way around these alternatives, but turn back to words, and question them again, and weigh them up? In the same way a tennis player, if he has just missed a shot, looks with surprise at a racket that is suddenly *separate* from him. And an incompetent workman becomes more distinctly aware of the tool he's using; a patient, of his body—to the point where he sees himself as being subjected to this body, to this tool, and as if he is their prisoner. What strikes us most about a language we only know a little is its methods and its tools, that is, its words; and about our own language, its ideas. But commonplace expressions, clichés and grandiose words, if they can at any moment lend themselves to two opposing ways of being *understood*, are a strange, almost double language, which at the same time we possess and do not possess. And what reader, if he has even the slightest concern for exactness, would not for that reason want to be rid of the dread, and the influence, of words and sentences? Neither Gourmont nor Albalat show us what it was like for Bourget when he wrote—but they show what happens with Albalat and Gourmont when they read Bourget. Marcel Schwob does not reveal the thoughts of the journalist, but the thoughts of Marcel Schwob when he reads his journal. And the criticism, finally, that we make of the flowers of rhetoric tells us something about the person spoken to, not the speaker, something about the reader, and not the author of clichés.

We might term *projection* the intellectual mechanism whereby we constantly transfer onto an object, an animal or a person the feeling that they cause us to experience. Thus marble seems cold to us, and a wool blanket, warm. A child who catches his fingers in a door imagines that the door intended to do it. The illusion is even more powerful when we are dealing with a person: someone who is shy feels that everyone is following him with their eyes. An egotist explains the most gratuitous things other people do as motivated by reasons of self-interest. A lover sees his mistress's love radiate out towards him. A partisan, to support his thesis, quotes such and such a fact, the truth of which seems to him blindingly obvious.

We should add that a reader always maintains that an author *intended* to say the very thing he hears: Otherwise he constructs the image—if he misunderstands, tries to feel his way between different meanings, and ends up grasping at words—of a bewildered author who is himself constrained by, and in a sense a victim of, language. So the little girl who is taken to London, for example, is impressed by the fact that the children there can *already* speak English. "They must work so hard!" she says. On such occasions an author and a reader, a speaker and the person spoken to, positioned as they are on either side of language's divide—just like a tapestry-maker at work, and a collector of tapestries—may sometimes see each other the other way around. It is because a writer has *not paid enough* attention to words that a reader thinks he is preoccupied with words, calculating, verbose. Whereas if, on the other hand, a writer had seen a cliché as a ready-made phrase—and thus been led to avoid it, or at least to modify it enough so as to make it clear in what sense he had chosen to use it—the reader would be able to abandon himself freely to the meaning, and to what the author had in mind. If Bourget seems to Gourmont to be preoccupied with words, it is not *despite* the fact that he abandons himself to his thoughts, it is *because* he abandons himself to them. Paul Valéry notes that "inspiration comes from the reader." That is certainly true—for the reader of Paul Valéry. And I imagine that composition, unity, and rules come "from the reader" of Rimbaud or Apollinaire. It could be expressed in the form of a proverb: *An author's thoughts are a reader's words, and an author's words are a reader's thoughts.*

One of the curious traits of projection is the following: The reader locates this extreme presence and concern about words at the *origin* of a sentence or an offending passage, whereas in reality it occurs for him—as it has for us—at the *end* of his effort. Thus the eyes of his mind, like the eyes of his body, naturally saw objects upside down (in space for the one, and in time for the other). Or to put it another way, just as you only have to apply upward pressure on your eyeball to make objects appear as if they are moving downwards, so the reader who starts out his analysis with meaning, and pushes upwards to the words he stumbles over, sees (or thinks he sees) the author going down from words towards meaning. The most common image we have of a rhetorician is of someone preparing and setting out his combinations of language, *before* pouring his thoughts into them.

The Illusion in More Detail

We might have suspected right from the outset that the "power of words," far from being a precise observation, was merely the effect of an illusion. Whatever scientific apparatus is later brought to bear upon this crude projection, we only need to examine the vulgar forms it takes to discover that the *word* it deals with is not the same as a word in a linguistic or grammatical sense: it is merely an absence, a refusal, a void. When Hamlet says "Words . . .," the young girl, "Beautiful sentences

..., " or the polemicist, "God, liberty, those grandiose words ..., " we ought not to understand them to say: Here are vowels and consonants, which are arranged so as to ... No. They mean "God does not exist ..." "Love, what a joke!" We pointed out a little while ago that we hardly ever talk of "words" if, for example, a father dies, or we win a prize of a million francs. This is no doubt true, since people who are against money or the family are rarer than atheists. But we might well imagine an anarchist who comes along and says: "All this talk of family is just sentences. Fortune is just a word." Verbalism is always someone else's thoughts. We call ideas we want nothing to do with *words,* just as we call policemen *pigs,* and our landlord a *shark.* It is merely an insult, upon which it would be pointless to base a theory of language and of the world. Many a philosopher, I am well aware, has praised Bergson for having "gone beyond language." But if we start out by taking as language what we have gone beyond, what is left of the praise?

If we reread Albalat, Schwob, or Gourmont more carefully, it would not be too difficult to show that they are constantly motivated and guided by a similar illusion. So we are struck not so much by their accord and self-assurance as by their tentativeness and their contradictions (of which the illusion is, after all, merely the translation and the simplest effect). As if Terror, which knows exactly what it is condemning, were only vaguely aware of the reasons for condemning it. Gourmont, who at first admonishes authors of commonplace expressions for their cowardice and laziness, complains later on about their "slow and patient labor of deception." Albalat claims that clichés are what a reader of any work retains most easily; he adds a little further on that everyone reads clichés mechanically, and without even noticing them. They sometimes say that commonplaces are neutral and inexpressive, and sometimes that they possess an "extraordinary communicative virtue," in one instance they "repel and disgust" us, but in another they please and charm us, sometimes they "reveal a raw and violent sensibility," and other times they are a sign of aridness and persistent abstraction.[2] There is, then, not one of these contradictory objections

2. Cf. the following: "[With clichés] words fail to strike any new poses that can be determined by an inner reality ... (Pierre Lasserre, *Les Chapelles littéraires,* 1920, p. 310) And: "In

that we cannot also observe in ourselves, we who at times complain (silently) about the writer of clichés that "He would do better not to bother and to talk like everyone else," and at other times that "It would be too much trouble for him to speak naturally and to call things by their name." So it is clearer than ever that we are dealing with a myth which everybody creates—or rather allows to grow—as they will, at the meeting point of two opposite *points of view,* according to the illusion of projection.

There is something indefinably flattering and gratifying about Terror. If a critic points out that a writer has surrendered to words and sentences, it makes him feel better ("It was all very well for rhetoric," he says, "to go on about flowers and rules. But the essential thing is . . ."). But then again, if he starts out by fabricating his objection and creating it from nothing, how could he not derive a certain satisfaction from his work? A sculptor or a painter, in order to convey better something that eludes our senses—an animal in flight or someone running—also combines in a single figure two consecutive postures, or *people,* which are in reality irreconcilable.

As far as the rules and laws that follow on from this go, they are doubtless neither more nor less justifiable than the kick a child aims at a door out of revenge. The fact remains that its effects are infinitely more serious if they give rise to the different postures and critical or literary works we have seen. (But we will come back to these effects.)

❦ ❦ ❦   All we had to do was to look in more detail at the sentiments we share about literature, the principles adduced from these sentiments,

---

a novel with a beginning that is as common as 'One radiant morning,' there may be real emotion." (Rémy de Gourmont, *La philosophie de Stendhal,* p. 38) Or: "An ordinary reader will feel more emotion in a sentence that is banal than in an original one . . ." (Rémy de Gourmont, *La philosophie de Stendhal,* p. 40) And: "It is [because the book is written in a banal style], and for this reason alone, that it makes no impact, and that we forget it as soon as we have read it." (Antoine Albalat, *L'Art d'écrire,* p. 76) Or even: "If we allow ourselves [ready-made expressions] once, we will allow ourselves to use them twice, then three times, and once we're on that slippery slope we let ourselves go, since it is easier to write using the same style as everyone else than it is to have a personal style." (Antoine Albalat, *L'Art d'écrire,* p. 76) And: "The overly persistent work of the tricksters must be destroyed like a spider's web." (Pierre Lasserre, *Les Chapelles littéraires,* p. 322) and the reasons behind those principles, to make a singular discovery: that these days when we come into contact with literature and with language, we are only able to know them, to appreciate them, and therefore also to continue them ourselves, thanks to a series of errors and illusions as crude as an optical illusion: a broken stick in the water, for example, or better still a rock which seems to move upwards behind a waterfall. Due to a series of illusions we could call optical illusions, since they are derived from the way a literary work appears to us, the view we take of it. Except a new problem then arises for us, which is that an illusion of the mind can go on, withstand experiences, generate an infinite number of systems and texts—whereas an optical illusion, on the contrary, is explained away as soon as it appears. It would be nothing short of ridiculous to conceive of a hydraulic theory based on the properties of rocks ascending behind waterfalls. But Terror, which is based on an illusion that is hardly less crude, has been able, oddly enough, to dominate our literature and even our thought.

CHAPTER 8

⚜ ⚜ ⚜ Terror Finds a Way of Justifying Itself

> It is easy to see that the statue of Marshall Ney combines
> two poses: His left hand and his legs are placed where
> they were at the moment the marshall drew his sword;
> his upper body, which should be bent forward, is instead
> straightened up at the same time as his right arm is rais-
> ing his weapon as a command signal. The lifelike quality
> of the statue results from this duality.
>
> —Rodin

Physicists often say that, as strict and rigorous as their method is, it can provide us with a coherent vision of the world, and one that allows us to get some purchase on it. They are, however, quite skeptical that it actually *resembles* the world. They note in this regard, firstly, that we can never entirely escape our thoughts—and there is nothing to prove that they resemble the outside world in any way. Secondly that the *scientific object* itself, being of our own making, would probably no longer exist if it were not for the presence of man. We are thus led to conjure up in our minds the vague image of an untouchable and silent universe.

Here we can point out our advantage. As difficult as commonplace expressions, ideas, and images can be, they at least come to us from a world that is not foreign. They are part of our world, in the same way that love or pity are. And the knowledge we have of them cannot be completely foreign to these feelings either.

There are several curious effects that follow from this.

In Which Terror Makes Itself Useful

We have had occasion to say (compelled by the need to be clear) that language was made up of words and ideas, which stand side by side and are joined together. Now it seems as if there is something strange about this joining together that is a constant source of debate for people and poses no end of problems for them, something having to do mostly with how *faithful* an expression is: They wonder whether language betrays or serves our thoughts, whether there are thoughts we cannot express, or words we cannot think, and whether language in the end guarantees *exactly* the communion between men it seems to promise. This then leads quite quickly to a concern about the origin of words, and whether there was not a Golden Age when they resembled their objects more closely than they do today . . . These are the kinds of common-sense questions that people ask, which are more metaphysical than those asked by metaphysics itself.

Let us put them aside for now. One shared necessity emerges at any rate out of this concern for faithfulness, one that is so consistently and so closely bound up with language that it would be hard to separate it out entirely: It is that people need an assurance—but an assurance is all they need—that this language is entirely *at their service,* and that there is no term that could potentially be obscure or confusing. We know how zealously writers, grammarians, or lexicologists get rid of the slightest hint of obscurity or ambivalence—to the point where they assume at the outset, and take as a kind of law, that every word has *its own* idea, every idea *its own* word.

This law is perhaps closer to wishful thinking than to actual observation, and more like a moral than a scientific law. But it is so constant that it is in itself a law, even if it does not express one. "Of all the different expressions that could convey a single one of our thoughts, there is only one that is right. We do not always come across it when talking or writing, but it is nonetheless true that it exists." So says La Bruyère, as do each and every one of us. As if it were a matter each time of getting the writer and the speaker to find the term that exactly expressed his thought—but of getting the reader or the person spoken to, to hear exactly that term, such that it is, even if for a fleeting moment, the most faithful reply and image possible of this writer and such that, ultimately, it seems as if between the two of them *there had been no language.*

Only who could now fail to see how effective and precise Terror seems to be when we consider it again from this point of view? Granted, it is a pure illusion if the writer of clichés is seen by his reader to be completely obsessed with words. The fact remains that the cliché is the place where this illusion *regularly* comes into play, following on from the cliché as if it were a natural effect. And it remains the case that the cliché, designated as such by the illusion, is the perfect place in language for the reader to completely lose sight of the writer—since he cannot tell if this writer has thought carefully about the cliché, or whether he has simply repeated it; this reader then imagines the author who surrenders entirely to thought as someone caught up in arranging words. The cliché is a place of non-understanding.

Now this danger must appear all the more serious to a scrupulous critic in that we are dealing with an expression whose invention is still close to us, visible, human. We see language betraying us before our very eyes, by introducing into speech, as an effect of its particular operation—and more precisely, as an effect of the ways in which repetition operates—the very obscurity and misunderstanding *it was designed to dispel.* This on its own would be bad enough, but we are dealing with a language that is still close to us, and with yesterday's mistake, which has not even quite been made yet. So if justice is to be done, commonplaces should be the first terms to be banished from a well-constructed language. In this sense, Terror keeps our original concern about faithfulness going, just as giving orders or expressing impatience—and even the way we sometimes say to hell with it—can prolong an initial request or a modest and persistent plea. The intention, at any rate, has not changed: as for the rest, we deal with the most urgent matters first, and how we do it, after all, is unimportant. If an astronomer persistently mistakes a defect in his telescope for a lake on the moon, he should get a new telescope. If commonplaces *regularly* throw readers into a state of ineffectuality and doubt, we should get rid of commonplaces once and for all. Instead of expressing indignation at Terror's methods and means, perhaps we ought to admire its wisdom.

A rather simplistic and crude wisdom, I agree. And one that too readily contents itself with the first argument that comes along. But then, supposing this argument was enough for what it was saying? Since the regular effect of the cliché is, in the optics of language, an illusion of projection, the simplest thing to do would be to agree that we recognize it in terms of that projection. After all, whether or not it is an illusion matters little, since all we want to do is *put an end* to it. And it is not just Terror's general approach that we would thus be led to acknowledge—or better still, to reinvent—but all of its rules and proofs, without which we would have trouble imagining it to be effective: these being difference, originality, and absence.

We have to take things further still, and question whether or not these rules are as illusory as they seemed.

In Which Terror Is Not Entirely Implausible

I admit that clichés could only have come to writers via one of the two routes we have seen: reinvention or habit (are there other routes?). A writer has had the chance to reread what he wrote, indeed probably had to—thus putting himself in the same position as the reader of his work. And I accept that his initial understanding of a commonplace expression will always prevail: It would be surprising if, when he read it over and tried it out, he did not feel at least some sense of the discomfort and hesitation that the reader is going to feel. It would be surprising, because a writer is someone whose purpose is to speak, to *express* himself with all of his tastes and passions, and to express those of people who remain silent: He is a *specialist* of expression, trained in different styles, and in the illusions of expression, someone who is familiar with every one of its features and contours, who yields to its imperatives. If he keeps such and such a cliché in his text, it is not out of simple ignorance; it is because he chooses to override the hesitation, either by neglecting it, or by trying to use it to some advantage: "They can interpret this any way they like! It's not my business any more, it's theirs"[1]—all of these will be seen by critics as examples of neglect or weakness that they will feel justified in holding against him.

We should, in fact, have already made a point of showing how crude and simplistic the distinction is that we started out with. Just as all readers occasionally allow themselves to be taken in, when reading, by the illusion that a poem or novel might have been written by them, so all writers, *a fortiori,* are able to read as if they were themselves a stranger—even if they hate doing so—and to see things, in turn, from the perspective of the author and the reader, of the person speaking and the person spoken to. And how could we not agree that Bourget or Carco, like us, *witnessed* their clichés, in accordance with the same illusion? So that they would be the first to admit that their texts originate in a certain subservience to words; and if by some chance this had not occurred to them, they would acknowledge it after the slightest reproach, being no less Terrorist than their critics. (Which doubtless explains why they usually fail to stand out.) Our mind is accustomed to these kinds of projections and reversals; this is precisely the way that, in a dream, the mind situates the noise that triggered them off at the end of its adventures; or even, when fully awake, the mind situates a clear vision of the successful (or failed) outcome of a project at its origin. Maury had enough time to dream fifty different episodes, all ending with him being led to the guillotine, before he woke up with his head caught under the wooden bar of his bed. We read in a newspaper: "Murdered for twenty francs"—as if the murderer had necessarily anticipated this amount of money, and as if he would not have been happy with, say, a thousand, or ten thousand francs. An author of clichés is thus the first person to *see* himself as a verbalist, as someone who is thrown to words. So Terror's grievance would not only be convincing: It would also stand a very good chance of *appearing* justified and well-founded—I am not saying this is patently clear for the person producing a cliché, but for the person enduring it. The mind has such great difficulty deluding itself completely once it has

---

1. Indeed, a writer often encourages this feeling in the reader. He offers him this bait, and makes him think he cannot do without him. This is the intention behind more than one apparently awkward expression in his work.

taken the wrong path, that it inevitably ends up *resembling* the error it has made.

Now the same remarks are equally valid for any example of the power of words. It is a myth if you like, but at least it is a useful myth: I see nothing wrong with rejecting (as this myth would like to) troublesome words, whose meanings are as diverse as *class, democracy, order,* or *freedom*—or at least with agreeing to stabilize their meaning. But this myth is one that also, at any given moment, becomes fact. It is not enough simply to believe in sirens for us to see them in the water, but it is certainly enough to believe in the influence of words for this influence to take effect immediately: and the least one can say about it is that this influence is clearly visible at any given moment. There are some words we like to repeat. There are others we are afraid of. During peacetime we avoid the word *war:* instead we say *national defense.* Instead of *devaluation,* we say *monetary alignment.* Instead of the words *an increase in the French deputy's allowance,* we say (painfully) *a coefficient taking into account the rise in the cost of living.* We say *diseased* rather than *syphilitic,* and *particular* rather than *diseased.* One political party avoids the word *order,* while another party avoids the word *freedom.* I am willing to accept that the power of words originates in an illusion. But an illusion that is so widespread, and whose success is always so immediate, hardly deserves to be called an illusion.

In Which Terror Appears Truthful

There is one other reason why we should question whether we have not overly exaggerated the seriousness of the error.

In what *precise* sense can we say that the word "*lamp*" *truly* denotes a lamp, and the words *house* or *Antares,* a house or the star Antares? All that's meant by this is that everyone has agreed to settle on a given meaning for these words, to the exclusion of any other meaning. We would perhaps like a star to *naturally* bear the name Antares, or for there to be some hidden resemblance between an actual lamp and the word *lamp,* based on its letters or its sounds—and this would certainly correspond to one of our deepest wishes. Further than that, it would correspond to an unspoken wish, to a certain vision of the world (or which thinks it is): "How do we know," a child asks, "that it is called Antares?" There is no shortage of philosophers who (like this child) impose a natural origin on language. Let us acknowledge at least that this origin normally remains hidden from us, and that the doctrine supporting it is unreliable. Even onomatopoeia, which at first seems to offer some proof of natural origins, is misleading. A word that is quite arbitrary becomes, as time goes by, an onomatopoeia: *trois muids* [three *muids*] transformed into *trémie* [grain container].[2] Conversely, any given onomatopoeia becomes arbitrary: *pipio* turns into *pigeon*. This is more or less the same degree of effectiveness we find with wishes. When we actually use it, our language is, with a few exceptions, quite arbitrary. But then, what is there to say about this *other part* of the meaning of a given word, or a given saying, namely that *there is always a certain anxiety about words and language*? And what right do we have—if it is the effect of a constant illusion, and itself a constant anxiety—to refuse meaning this additional element, or signification this additional detail? If clichés do have one predictable trait, it certainly seems to us to be a linguistic nuance. It is no doubt true that "mysterious-languor" denotes a certain kind of languor: but not without also alluding in some way to the words themselves. And if a "habit which governs" really refers to nothing more than a habit, this reference is at least *accompanied by language.* One key element of "frivolous-life-of-man-about-town," and equally of abstract terms like *freedom, constitution,* and *justice,* is that a certain power of words seems to be at work in them. And if we accept everything else, what right do we have to refuse this following stage, this natural nuance, since at least *it seems to provide us with a preliminary justification*? What a strange field of inquiry, in which objects immediately conform to the way we see them, and where predictable illusions turn out to be more true than invisible truths.[3]

---

2. [A muid is an old measure of cubic capacity, equivalent to about 1,000 liters. It was commonly used to measure corn, hence the etymology of *trémie,* a large grain container, the capacity of which might have been 3000 liters. *Trans.*]

3. Likewise, if we allow ourselves to take the theories of people like Marx and Sorel lightly, it is not in order to see them as being motivated by *misology.* Quite the opposite. It is likely that Freud's discoveries, for example, are a little bit truer today than they were at first. (The critique of language simply provides the means for going beyond them.)

Should we still be surprised that Terror remains as forceful and assertive as ever? No, if all we need to do is to subject its doctrine to the most basic requirement—indeed, what would a language be if it were not used to express and communicate, and could we still call it a language?—in order to determine its effectiveness; to say it is plausible would be an understatement: it is valid and true insofar as it is formulated and thought out. So it is natural to conclude that we would only need to think it out *a little bit more*—forcefully, and ruthlessly—in order to make it even more valid and true: with a truthfulness that is finally indisputable, and free from all doubt. This approach would enable us to hunt down and get rid of, even more vigorously than Terror did, the merest hint of anxiety about language—to constantly put on trial even the least used phrases and the most natural words . . .

All we need to do. We already know what we are bound to meet if we follow this path. We, too, are led toward absence, revolt, and infinite deprivation. Would anyone regret it, if this is the price to pay for a perfect transaction? "No seemingly beautiful or perfect work is worth it," the poet says to himself, "if it is not at the cost of an extreme exactness, or a successful communion—even if it is only for a single moment, or a single word, and even if it never returns. In that fleeting moment, at least, I have been you."

⚜ ⚜ ⚜   Is Terror derived any less from an illusion? Definitely not. But we should simply see it as an opportunity for admiring the way in which our mind—although not correcting with any precision the illusion to which it is subjected, but on the contrary wearing it out and pushing it as far as it will go—is able to create, out of its very defects and flaws, the most favorable environment for the free play of communication and reflection. Rather than the rock which appears to rise behind the waterfall (and does not), we should think instead of the kinetoscope and the cinema, and the *truthfulness* of the illusory duration of visual images on the retina. Terror, too, can now look to us more like an art or a technique than a science.

It remains to be seen whether, on the specific point that concerns us, it is the most skillful art, or the most effective technique.

CHAPTER 9

❦ ❦ ❦ Terror Fulfilled

> Balzac's grandiloquence is only a game,
> because he is never fooled by it.
> —Joubert's notebooks

We said that an excessive preoccupation with language revealed a short-circuit of meaning between author and reader. We were, however, forced to acknowledge a little later on that this opposition of author to reader—of someone speaking and someone spoken to—was strictly one of convenience. There is no absolute difference between the conversations we have with everyone else, and the secret conversation that we all have with ourselves. Every author is also *his* own reader, every speaker *his* interlocutor—such that Terror raises (and resolves, in its own way) the problem not only of literature and its authenticity, but also of how we communicate with ourselves: of how we think.

Literature no doubt uses its own more sensitive scales, and more precise forms of measurement—which are more rigorously demanding. In any case the overriding problem is the most serious of all, if it is posed, and demands to be resolved, with every single thought we have. And which of us does not feel that there might exist a kind of Terror *between ourselves and ourselves* which, rather than risking vagueness and inexactness, rushes blindly into[1] hermeticism, exclusivity, or absence—only leaving behind, between ourselves and ourselves, the briefest of flashes. (But maybe this Terror, too, is capable of making some progress).

---

1. ["se jette à esprit perdu dans." Paulhan is here playing neologistically on the idiomatic French expression *se lancer à corps perdu,* to rush headlong into something, and *perdre ses esprits,* to take leave of one's senses. *Trans.*]

A Few Technical Faults

What we need to do, so as to quickly see what they are, is to consider Terror's *faults:* By this I mean the points at which it betrays itself, and reveals itself to be different from the image it presents to us.

It may have seemed to us at first, when we saw how carefully Terror distinguished between pure and impure sentences, that it possessed all the hallmarks of intellectual probity, sound analysis, and discrimination. Yet it would now appear to us, on the contrary, to be simplistic and generalized. There are thousands of clichés which are not open to the slightest doubt or uncertainty of meaning: it is *as clichés* that we understand them. Who still sees a ship in *the ship of state,* or a heart in the *heart of a gathering?* There is no error in them to fear, no illusion to correct. On the contrary, whenever certain proverbs or sayings are used appropriately—as is the case among rural folk, or within a political party, or even within a family—we see the speakers agreeing on the general sense of an expression, and constantly using clichés without ever stumbling over their language. But in order to avoid a cliché which might possibly be misunderstood, Terror ends up ruining a hundred others which would be perfectly comprehensible.

In the same way, a schoolteacher keeps an entire class behind after school because of one guilty child who has not confessed; and the sign forbids all flowers after one of them has been stolen. It may well be that the urgency and the difficulties of an investigation sometimes make such measures acceptable. But it won't escape people's notice that we should reflect on the fact that Terror can at least take *all of its time,* that it is dealing with a *predictable* danger, of which it would not be impossible to undertake a permanent investigation, and offer a kind of information service; and that nothing would be easier than *to decide* in advance on the meaning of any uncertain elements of a commonplace expression. But we'll leave this for now.

There is a second fault, which is no less obvious than the first one. Terror first appeared to us as full of initiative and perpetually vigilant, ready to eliminate mercilessly the slightest weakness, the merest concession to language. Now what strikes us, on the contrary, is its inertia and passivity.

There is one practical way of avoiding contagious illnesses: that is to get rid of those who are ill—or at least to keep them permanently isolated. There is a way of fighting which consists in dodging punches (or at least in knowing how to take them). But there is another, wiser method, which consists in anticipating the problem: either by throwing the first punches, or by isolating and getting rid of, one by one, the causes of leprosy or tuberculosis. Now Terror, in the war it wages against an affliction of language, behaves like a doctor who would execute any patients suffering from contagious illnesses—in the same way that a barbarian warrior waits until he is struck before he puts his hand up to the place where he is wounded. Terror is no doubt vigilant in eliminating suspect expressions and words, those it sees as already infected by a kind of disease and liable to produce a short-circuit of meaning—thus placing its anxiety and all of its energy *after* the error (to which it has resigned itself). But we should reflect on the fact that with commonplace expressions we are dealing with a vice that is so *predictable,* that it would not be impossible to imagine an equally predictable initiative that could prevent it from occurring. (Just as, in a closely related field, grammars and dictionaries do. Their concern is less to condemn incorrect usage of meanings and phrases—which they would have to do with every word—than to *decide on and fix* the right meaning for them).

There is a third fault, which is no less appreciable. This is that Terror is verbal, and more preoccupied with language than rhetoric has ever been. We had occasion earlier to remark that Terrorist writers, even though of all the authors they have the keenest desire to avoid the reproach of verbalism, are also the first to attract this reproach. We can now understand the reason for this. For Terror is above all dependent upon language in a general sense, in that it condemns a writer to say only what a certain *state* of language leaves him free to express: He is restricted to those areas of feeling and thought where language has not yet been overused. That is not all: No writer is more preoccupied with words than the one who at every point sets out to get rid of them, to get away from them, or to reinvent them. Even that is not all, since he sets out to *prove* that he has reinvented them, and to provide the evidence of his innocence. Now this evidence, however fluid and subtle we would like it to be, and even when it is faulty and breaks down, is itself linguistic in nature. It is *other words* which prove that we have escaped from words. Which is why a Surrealist poem is easier to imitate than a classical sonnet. In undertaking this adventure, Terrorist writers make one think, curiously, of Gribouille, who jumps into the water in order to get out of the rain.

Here again, it is hard to resist imagining a technique that would be more effective than Terror, and that would prevent this obsession with language in a writer. There is a way of fighting mosquitoes which consists of slapping yourself hard as soon as you have been bitten. Besides the fact that it comes too late and is very crude, the inconvenience of this method is clear, which is that it does the same as a mosquito (only more violently). But there is a more subtle and foresightful means of protection, which is to spread oil over the surface of the water. It might be time, in our attempts to protect ourselves against an illusion that is more dangerous to the mind than an insect bite and fever are to the body, to turn from the slapping system to the oil system.

A Method of Prevention

Many a time Terror, because of its abrupt and simplistic reactions, its blindness, and its intolerance, may have reminded us of some mental illness. But maybe in one respect it is more like a neurosis, namely in the pretexts it uses as a cover: apparently free and bold, when it is in fact a slave; subtle, when it is crude; and lastly, effective, when it is inert. It is literature in its wild state, whereas it presents itself as the last word on progress. In the same way as an illusionist, in a suspicious gesture, draws attention to the side of the table where *nothing is happening,* a neurosis likewise hides its weakness, and presents itself as something it is not—so that one's efforts to overcome it are all wrong, and simply make it stronger and more coherent. This is how critics have greatly strengthened Terror, since they agree with it that the weight of words is crushing, but admonish it for its excessive freedom, its boldness, and the dangers it presents to morality and society. Romanticism has doubtless had no more powerful (even if hidden) supporters than Pierre Lasserre and the Neo-Classicists.

It is odd that we have until now neglected the aspect of Terror by which it first appeared to us. And our neglect was no doubt because of the extreme *obviousness* of that aspect. This obviousness can no longer fool us, though.

Terror began by reminding us, as if it were self-evident, that clichés are superfluous, since everyone already knows them and uses them. Straight away, it added that there is nothing people are usually more in agreement about than what is banal and stupid. It's so stupid and such a cliché, people say. All an author was doing, in short, was showing how stupid he was.

It would be all too easy to reply that there are startling proverbs, and ingenious clichés; that such and such a thought, even though it is common, is not however lacking in sharpness or finesse. We could argue that we normally only quote obvious statements, moreover, in order to communicate others that are not obvious, and that a saying as banal as "there is no smoke without fire" can be used in thousands of different subtle or paradoxical ways in a conversation. And so on. We could go on for pages and pages, and Terror is no doubt particularly adept at provoking to its advantage one of the discussions in which men are most willing to engage. (Who does not enjoy arguing about intelligence and stupidity?) To its advantage: For we can now see all too clearly that this would be to fall into the most deceptive trap that it could set for us. I have no idea whether commonplace expressions are intelligent or stupid, and I cannot see any way of ever finding out in a rigorous manner. But one thing we can say for sure is that *they are not common,* despite their name, and despite their appearance. On the contrary, if they have one characteristic trait—and which is the source of the faults we have seen, from inertia to confusion—it is that they are an exceptionally vacillating and diverse form of expression, one that lends itself to being understood in two, even four, different ways, and a kind of monster of language and reflection.[2] It lends itself to all sorts of trickery, justifying all manner of defenses (even the one

---

2. Thus, for anyone who receives it as a thought, it is sometimes as picturesque and detailed as a little tale, and sometimes more concentrated and drier than an abstract idea. But for anyone who hears it as a sentence, it is conventional or new, and so on.

which invokes the myth of powerful words) . . . But we are no doubt dealing with a truth so dangerous to Terror that it needs all the tricks and traps it can to hide it.

At least we have finally identified it, and have found the permanent investigation we need to set up, the technique we need to discover, and the fear we need to cast aside—the water upon which to pour the oil. Clichés may once again take up residence in literature the day they are at last deprived of their ambiguity and their confusion. Now all it should require, since the confusion stems from a doubt as to their nature, is simply for us to *agree,* once and for all, to accept them as clichés. In short, we simply need to *make* commonplace expressions *common*—and along with them those larger scale commonplaces: literary rules and norms, rhetorical figures, dramatic unities, which are all subject to the same fortunes and obey the same laws. We would perhaps need, at most, a few lists and some commentary; and to get started, a bit of goodwill, and a simple decision. Who could refuse it, if they remained faithful to the same desire to be understood and to communicate which secretly motivated Terror, and which here is pursued out in the open?

Some people might say that a method that is appropriate for larvae and microbes is not necessarily appropriate for words. This is true. But the difference between them works to our advantage. We cannot make mosquitoes disappear simply by imagining an earth without mosquitoes. But just as words immediately became powerful simply because we imagined a power of words, all we have to do to dispel this power, no doubt, is to stop imagining it. Where an illusion creates a fact, disillusion will ruin it. If a cliché is seen precisely to be common, it is no more likely than any other term to cause the least anxiety about words or their power. If there is one field in which the method of prevention should be completely effective, it is this one, and perhaps this one alone.

Rhetoric or, Terror Perfected

There are thousands of examples, without even looking beyond Terror, which prove that the technique we are dreaming of is sufficient—insofar as it dispels the illusion of a power of words, or rather, prevents it from occurring—to give back the use of rhyme to poets, the benefits of dramatic unities to playwrights, and the use of commonplace expressions to all.

We could already have made the following observation: Terrorists, who are in such a hurry to proscribe clichés, have no hesitation in using them as *titles:* In fact, it seems that they are on the contrary as triumphant (even aggressive) *in this place* as they were elsewhere shameful and despicable. Jean Cocteau calls his collections of essays *Carte blanche, Secret professionnel* [Professional secrets]. Breton calls his *Point du Jour* [Break of Day], *Les Pas Perdus* [The Lost Steps]. Aragon calls his poems *Feu de joie* [Bonfire], *Le Mouvement perpétuel* [Perpetual motion]. Paul Morand calls his *Feuilles de température* [Temperature chart]; Drieu la Rochelle calls his *État-civil* [Civil status]. What is the difference? Well, it is that because they are titles, and highlighted, that these writers are consistently *aware* of them, and use them for what they are.

We could imagine a thousand other instances: irony, insistence, a slight distortion, a subtle displacement, a lowering of voice.[3] By creating a kind of self-reflexive zone around clichés, they are sufficient to let us know that "it's safe," that we are in no danger of being fooled, and that we and the author are *on the same side* of the commonplace expression: "A devoted woman of limited intelligence who, imbued with a sense of duty (as the saying goes), had finished a mother's first obligation toward her daughters . . ."[4] Another example: "The Seine, still more or less calm, was sadly enjoying the peacefulness before the flags, the pennants, the fanfare."[5] But we now know that we are in a position to further extend this complicity, this pleasure, to cover all of literature.

This pleasure . . . more than pleasure, really: a certain *quality.* We had occasion to observe (not without regret nor unease, and as if language

---

3. Few writers have exploited these nuances as skillfully as Goethe. In terms of writing conventions, we should also mention the italics, the quotation marks, and the parentheses which we see proliferate in Romantic writers as soon as rhetoric is invalidated.

4. Balzac.

5. Léon-Paul Fargue.

were failing in one of its duties) that every word, or just about every word, was for us arbitrary. This is also the nostalgia Terror usually feels, haunted by the idea that language was once innocent and direct, that there was a Golden Age when words *resembled* things, when each term was *named*, each word was "accessible to all the senses."[6] Such that no power of words would be able to creep in, since all words would be transparent. Who among us is not moved by this thought? And yet it is down to us to obtain such a language. For there is not one commonplace expression—nor line of poetry, or rhyme, or genre—*from the moment we accept it as such*—that does not belong to this language, and is not this very word. We are not in a position to know why *languor* denotes languor. But it is easy to understand that *mysterious-languor* denotes a kind of languor: All we need to do is, first of all, hear it as a cliché, as if it were a single word, and then to hear it as two words, as if it were an opinion. And to understand that *secret-professionnel* is a sort of secret, *pas-perdus* a room, *point-du-jour* a dawn. Eyes melt, love grows, a road disappears, and we are thrown into this state of wonder, in which the poet's thought, without ever stumbling over words, goes from idea to idea, from passion to passion, in this more purified air: an expression which is infinitely transparent to the mind. For once again, Terror's only real regret—as is the case with neuroses—is for the kind of feeling that it had at first attempted to destroy.[7]

We should be surprised that a technique which offers us such tangible pleasure, and such immediate benefits, has never before been invented. But the fact is that is has been invented. It has existed, it exists, and is so durable that we should perhaps take it as a law, of which Terror is merely an exception. Let us get back to what we were talking about.

---

6. Rimbaud.

7. We are talking here about an imperative which is too vigorous, no doubt, not to break through here and there despite everything, even if, for want of a commonplace, it has to content itself with resorting to etymology (whether it is exact or not is of little importance). In fact, there is a certain use of the words *scruple, candid, apprehension,* or *to be on the point of* [être au point de] ("It was because I did not know what voluptuousness was, and had as yet no apprehension of pleasure . . ." [André Gide]); "And at the golden point of dying [*au point doré de périr*]," [Paul Valéry]), which are apt to give us a foretaste of the kind of rapture that no cliché, law, or genre would now be able to withhold.

The art I am imagining would naïvely admit that we talk, and write, in order to make ourselves understood. It would add that there is no more troubling obstacle to this communion than a certain anxiety about words. Then, that it is difficult to do anything about this anxiety once it is there, when it takes on the appearance of a myth; but that it is on the contrary expedient to take precautions, and prevent it from occurring. *Run away from language and it will come after you. Go after language and it will run away from you.* Taking this as our point of departure, we would then quote and describe in detail all the different commonplace expressions, arguments, and rhetorical figures. Following which, we would see that we had solved the main linguistic difficulties that Terror claimed were unavoidable stumbling blocks for all writers. In short, we would have substituted a shared Rhetoric (to which these pages would be a fairly good introduction) for the dust of the different parties and individual rhetorics that Terror alludes to, in its solitude and its anguish.

Rhetoric, indeed. It is no longer a word that frightens us. If it has required so much effort to finally imagine and rather weakly describe this most ancient of arts—and the art that the Chinese and the Hindus themselves never thought could some day let literature down—the blame does not lie with us, but with Terror alone, and with how disreputable it has made the thing (so that rhetoric is no longer taught in the classroom), and the word (so that it has become synonymous with *verbose* and *bombastic*).

But we have now gone beyond Terror. Better still, we have *perfected* it—forcing its peculiarities, its taboos, and its tricks to the point where it dissolves back into an old and joyful science. Lord Kelvin only accepted as natural facts those that he was able to reproduce in his laboratory. Likewise, it is in our own laboratory that the great event of literature has just been played out: this passage from collections of hackneyed sayings to Rhetoric, and from Terror to Maintenance—and in which the history of literature is not the only interested party.

❦ ❦ ❦   I've no idea if it was really necessary to stray off down so many little tracks and across so much undergrowth in order to find an old royal road again. I needed to, is all I can say. (I suppose I have to confess here that I was, all along, a Terrorist). It is a peculiar situation to be in when you discover, after so much effort, what everyone has always known. Peculiar, but not unpleasant. Innocent Fèvre, in order to rekindle the joy he sadly felt he had lost in being at home, would enter his bedroom from the roof. We have been across many a roof.

That said, I may possibly have been exaggerating. When all is said and done, rhetoric has never stopped existing, since Terror has also never stopped condemning it. And although the more delicate forms such as syllepsis or hypallage have disappeared, neither *commonplace,* nor *subject,* nor *composition* are words devoid of meaning for us. We could say, rather, that Terror here again acts a bit like a neurosis—which allows someone afflicted by it to be a good spouse or a good citizen, of course, but not without a certain profound lack, not without his life being deeply marked by a hidden crystallization of the neurosis, which threatens at any moment to affect the healthy part. Similarly, Terror cannot prevent regular lines of poetry, or the happiness we get from simple tales. It can never quite prevent joy, or grandeur. It simply gives its victims a bad conscience, and that fear of being fooled which makes fools of us. But we have now been liberated from that.

CHAPTER 10

❦ ❦ ❦ A Device to Reverse the Direction of Literature

Man is a wet knife: If you don't wipe the blade and
handle dry every day, it's not long before it gets rusty.
—Bara proverb

I have tried to improve the Terrorist method without taking away any of
its rigor. What has happened, though, is that instead of making it more
refined or nuanced, I have in a sense *redoubled it:* applying a parallel
analysis not only to the author, but also to the reader, not only to the
speaker, but also to the person spoken to.

We ought to have been able to anticipate the danger of such a pro-
cedure: that its object disappears, and a commonplace expression essentially becomes impossible to grasp, if it can take on equally one or
the other of two opposing figures. Its truth eludes us, so that it is less
a question of knowing it scientifically, than of *doing* it, and of keeping
its nature simple by using the techniques of art.

Indeed, this fault is (it seems) inevitable, and all we can do is to ac-
commodate it, if we cannot hope to repair it. We have in fact seen the
curious benefit to be derived from this technique, and the seriousness
of the example it sets for the writer, who is condemned to recreate a
heavenly language for us. It remains for us to insure it a little better,
and to protect it with a few guarantees.

The Critic and the Elephant

Baudelaire advises eccentric writers, if they wish to cast off their ec-
centricity (or at the very least to make it invisible), that they should
pursue it: They should push it as far as it will go. This is what we have

done. We have pushed Terror as far as it will go, and have discovered Rhetoric.

A different rhetoric, to be sure, from what we usually understand by this word. But not so different that we cannot easily undo the illusion that people commonly have about it. The hand-rail that is erected at the edge of an abyss by a foresighted mayor could give a traveler the impression that his freedom is being infringed upon. The traveler is wrong, of course. All he would need to jump, if he really wants to, would be a little bit of energy. And in any case the hand-rail allows him to get closer to the abyss, and to see its every nook and cranny. Rhetoric is just the same. We may have the impression, from a distance, that its rules are going to guide a writer's hand—that it holds him back, at any rate, from abandoning himself to the stormy emotions of his heart. But the fact is that it allows him, on the contrary, to give himself up to them without restraint, since he is freed from the whole apparatus of language which was in danger of being confused with these emotions.

We should have been able to notice this sooner, and without making such a fuss about it.

There is one aspect of Terror which ought not to surprise us: that is how wrong its critics are. The minute a critic finds literary genres, dramatic unities and commonplace expressions despicable, and the only works worthy of respect those that surprise and disconcert, there is just one resource left to him if he wants to express his admiration: Whether he confesses to being surprised, disconcerted, or confused, he should be so *truthfully,* and should be outraged. The mistake that Sainte-Beuve, Brunetière, Lemaître, and Faguet make, is that their doctrine only allows them to pay one single sort of homage to Balzac, Baudelaire, Nerval, and Zola. And in this, they have not let us down.

When Fabre described how carefully the sacred scarab beetle mixes and kneads the pill in which it encloses its egg, he added rather curiously that the organs of this insect seemed to be made for an entirely different activity, and that there is nothing they could be less well equipped for than mixing and kneading. "The idea that comes to my mind," he says, "is of an elephant that would like to make lace." The same could be said of critics. I want each of their constructions to be ingenious and plausible. Their doctrines gradually ruin them, though, and undermine them from the inside; in the end they are left with nothing to show for themselves but uncertainty and contradiction when confronting an authentic work of literature. Indeed, this is what they have secretly wanted. They have chosen to be elephants.

There is one aspect of this secret that should have been revealed to us earlier on by a fairly clear contradiction in the way they go about things. Because they clamor for novelty. That's all well and good. (And we can wisely assign literature the task of revealing a part of man and the world that science cannot reach.) What is more serious, though, is that they clamor for *any kind of* novelty: whether in man or his passions and his instincts, or in terms of style itself and its images. Now only one of these demands can be acceptable: What is surprising is that anyone could formulate them all at the same time. For each of them is only satisfied if one renounces all the others. In order for the subject of a novel to appear to us as new, its language still has to be neutral enough not to draw attention to itself.[1] In order for an image to appear to us as unexpected, the two objects it brings together still have to be familiar. We can be moved by the sight of a flying horse, because we already have a familiar, almost commonplace, idea of a horse and of wings. If the horse itself were astonishing to us in every respect, we would be no more surprised to see it fly than run. "Do you expect," asks a naïve author, "a new ideal from me? Tell me, then, what sort of man you would intend it to be for." "Well, we would also like a new kind of man." "All right, then tell me the passions I should use to make up this new man." "Why, passions we have never heard of." "And what about his instincts?" "Be sure and discover them while you're at it." "You'd want them at least to be truthful, and ordinary?" "No. Man's errors, his fantasies, his follies, are just as good as the truth." "And what if I happened to follow public opinion?" "We would at least require a new style." "Why don't you just admit what you're thinking: It is not so much style, or instinct, or passions that you are keen on, as *difference,*

---

1. We all know how difficult it is to appreciate, and even to grasp, the plot of a novel written in an "artistic style."

of any kind, and you are less concerned to learn about the world and man than you are to unlearn them."

But we now hold the key to this strange imperative, and to the confusion that ensues. What Terror wants is not so much for a writer to be inventive, different, or unique, but for him to express himself and to make himself understood *in spite of* his difference. How difficult this expression will be to achieve—and thus how worthy of merit—is in direct proportion to how unusual the author is. So during periods of Terror, literature happily welcomes, and even seeks out—just as in sport people sometimes seem to get behind a misshapen champion, a bowlegged runner, a consumptive cyclist—mad poets or absurd thinkers, those small or great Satans of the quill.

Let us imagine, though, that we have exorcised once and for all any haunting fears, and taken language in hand—that Rhetoric has replaced the various dictionaries of sayings, and Maintenance replaced the different forms of Terror. Only then could the imperative, of which Terrorists only provided us with a caricature, at last be given free rein—and critics could stop being elephants. If I want someone to confide something in me, I don't ask them to tell me it in a language that takes me by surprise: The simplest words are all that are needed. The same is true of literature: If its originality should be in what it reveals about a person, it has everything to gain by adopting already accepted subjects and ideas. Just as two men conversing in the same language do not so much lose their personalities in this language as they reveal them, and in a way give birth to them, so the same can be said of two writers who express themselves using fixed genres and common themes. Phèdre is what *distinguishes* Racine from Pradon, just as Amphitryon is what distinguishes Molière from Plautus.

A Rhetoric Which Does Not Speak Its Name

We should have asked ourselves honestly whether we had not painted rather a black picture of Terror. After all, neither rebellion nor absence, neither monsters nor emotional outbursts are necessarily terrorist—and inspiration was not invented yesterday. If Byron is feverish, Pascal is no less so. La Fontaine is sometimes possessed, and Jammes absent to himself. Le Cid is more exotic than Ruy Blas, and Bajazet than the Natchez. Racine writes about princesses just as much as Victor Hugo does about prostitutes, but of the two, princesses are the rarer. Corneille and Boileau (according to them) are only interested in expressing things that are exceptional, that have never been said before, that are surprising. Fénelon quarrels with his words just as much as Joyce does. We should have wondered, finally, asking the question with the utmost loyalty—and this might perhaps have led us to no longer ask it at all—whether literature, throughout all the different forms of Terror and Maintenance, has not always, across the ages, had the same choices, and the same preferences. But we now have an answer to this question as well.

Which is, more or less, that Corneille or Boileau are able to forgo novelty, whereas it is indispensable for Baudelaire or Victor Hugo if they want to express themselves at all. "I am proposing," says one of them, "my *non tam meliora quam nova* [there is nothing better than the new]." But the other: "There can be no art without surprise." Corneille is free to be new, even extravagant—because for him, in rhetorical terms, a cliché and a paradox are equivalent. But Baudelaire is not free, if a paradox alone is what for him confers meaning and dignity; Nerval *has* to hang himself, and Hölderlin go mad. Likewise for the others: Being feverish is for Pascal accidental, whereas for Byron it is a way of life. And Victor Hugo writes about prostitutes as a declaration of his principles: They carry a message. Whereas for Racine, princesses are seen as pure clichés, insofar as they are ruled by unbridled passion. For the former, it is because they are prostitutes; for the latter, despite the fact that they are princesses. And even personal style is for La Bruyère and Marivaux only one from among a hundred qualities—and certainly not as important as taste, composition, or the concern for authenticity. But for Schwob and Gourmont, as they freely admit, personal style is the very reason for, and the origin of, all the other qualities. Théramène's monster is as funny as a crocodile, but Surrealist monsters are every bit as boring as a scientific demonstration.

We could spell this aspect and this difference out more clearly: Rhetoric only sees feverishness and novelty as one of the events that a writer deals with. But Terror sees them as the means to these other events, and as the form they take. We could thus say that a work's *foundation*, its system of expression—or, if you like, its rhetoric (in the commonly accepted sense of the word)—is hidden from view as far as *Maintenance* is concerned, like the skeleton of a mammal, but is exposed as far as Terror is concerned, like the shell of a crustacean. Théophile Gautier wears his on the outside, like a lobster. But Racine's is on the inside, like a bull. A classical work of literature is free to offer us events, passions, and things themselves. But a Romantic work only presents these to us mingled with opinions, with methods and means, in other words mixed into literature. A Rhetorician makes his position on language clear once and for all, and is thereafter free to talk about love or fear, slavery or freedom. But a Terrorist cannot help mixing a constant concern about language and expression into his fear, love or freedom. Ruined castles, distant lights in the night, ghosts, and dreams (for example) are for the whole Romantic movement—which Surrealism has given a new and forceful lease of life—simple conventions, like rhyme and the three dramatic unities. But this does not *prevent* people from also seeing these conventions as dreams and castles, whereas no one has ever claimed to have seen the three unities. A prostitute resembles an actual prostitute, and a beggar a real beggar. This is the lie to which a writer is bound by all forms of Terror. It is not that language is any less present, but he cheats, and does not admit that it is language. We are surprised to see how bitterly each literary school nowadays complains about rival schools, about their conventions and their verbalism. What is even more surprising is that they are all right.

Consequently Terror requires, in order to be properly understood, a more alert critic than Rhetoric does, and a more obliging one—a reader who agrees to be an author's second-in-command, and who consents, if he wishes to accede to things themselves, to make his way through an endless series of passageways and edifices. Now, this task is not always easy. It can even seem quite disagreeable. "Show me all the monsters you like," said Chamfort. "Just don't lead me off into the wings." "We will drag you back there," Terror replies. A reader, or a critic, feels the same sense of mystification as an honest and innocent spectator feels when thinking about the wings. Brunetière finds fault (first of all) with Baudelaire, Lemaître with Mallarmé, France with Verlaine, Sarcy with Barrès, and Souday with Jules Romains, because of what they see as their bizarre sense of humor. A Terrorist will thus attract readers who are perhaps more fanatical—because they have to be more committed—than a Rhetorician, but he will attract less of them. If you go from Proust's *Le Temps Retrouvé* [*Time Regained*] to Joyce's *Ulysses,* from *Ulysses* to Péguy's *Les Tapisseries* [Tapestries], and from the *Les Tapisseries* to Gide's *Faux-Monnayeurs* [*The Counterfeiters*], you are not so much changing from one subject or atmosphere to another, as you are changing (painfully) from one entire *vision* and poetic art to another.

Yet we are also witnessing in our time the triumph and global appeal of the only genre that obeys rules stricter than Voltaire's tragedies and Malherbe's odes. I am thinking of that type of novel which proscribes from its range of emotions dreams, reveries, premonitions; from its choice of characters, metaphysicians, occultists, members of secret societies, Hindus, Chinese, Malaysians, twins; from its explanations, myths, allusions, symbols; from its figures of style, metaphors and ellipses—and which follows so rigorous an order in its narrative progression that it gives us in the very first chapter *all* the elements (characters, places, objects) of a problem that will not be resolved until the final pages.

We can now extend to all of literature this gesture toward reconciliation offered to us by the detective novel.

A Law of Expression

We said that Maintenance was more effective than Terror (and Rhetoric than anthologies of sayings). But it is also more *true.* For a Terrorist cannot prevent himself being duped. He *has* to assume, as he is arranging his meagre collection of words, that he is reinventing the world and man. The more he is a laborer and a meticulous technician, the more he has to *believe himself* to be a metaphysician, a general, a pope. Thereby constantly at fault, constantly *wrong* about the meaning and nature of his every enterprise, he never stops mistaking words for things, and things for words. But we now understand what it is that turns us away from one or the other error.

It is, first of all, that our monk (and our man who is unable to speak) need only speak *more willingly* if he wants his accent, and his embarrassment, to disappear: He need only *accept* his language. Or rather, if we think of the example of hunger: the movement itself of rushing toward the plainest of meals renders them exquisite; or makes those that have been thoroughly chewed over seem fresh and untouched. If our experience has any meaning, it is to show that the flaw we take clichés to task for—with all the wisdom in the world—ceases to exist as soon as we stop criticizing them. In short, Terror seems to be *a way of doing things* rather than an observation—and it is not because commonplace expressions are despicable that Terror proscribes them; it is because it proscribes them that they become despicable. It is as if there were no *pure* observation of language, as if a play of reflections and mirrors constantly revealed to us in language (and in literature) the reflection itself of the movement by which we approached it. Thus we become attached to our friends, and we see them as affectionate, more in relation to the things we do for them, than in relation to the things they do for us. And similarly people say that the surest way of making a young woman (or a garden, or an institution) loveable, is to love her. Or of making a thief honest, to trust him. But why so many examples, and of such dubious value as far as our experience is concerned?

We have followed this experience on one and then the other level respectively: on the one hand discovering that a writer has only to be afraid of and to steer clear of verbalism in order to find himself thrown right into the thick of it—as if our suspicion alone presented some danger: just as with those afflictions such as tremulousness, anxiety, or aerophagia, where the idea alone of them is somewhat perilous. And on the other hand we have discovered that all of those good things that Terror yearns for in its confused way, this virgin contact and these new meanings, all of this awaits us if we dare to rush at the ghost that fear conjures up before our eyes. Of course literature makes us uneasy if it is literary, the novel if it is novelistic, or the theatre if it is theatrical. But there is a way we can turn this unease to our advantage, which is to make theatre *a bit more* theatrical, the novel violently novelistic, and literature in general more literary.[2] All it requires is an enthusiastic impulse. All it requires is a reconciliation and a yes.

If I try to determine more clearly the principle governing this reconciliation, I have a sense first of all of some law of language which Terrorists stumble over, while Rhetoricians yield to it. Consequently the law, in return, powerfully serves the latter and takes them beyond their original limits, but it repels the former. *Volentem ducit, nolentem trahit* [It leads the willing, and drags along the unwilling].[3] But we must remind ourselves of the details of our success.

We said that it was necessary to distinguish within every word a part that is matter and a part that is spirit, which are joined to each other. If there was one aspect of literary expression—the commonplace—that seemed crucial to us (since it offered, in a condensed form, all of the characteristics of the different genres, rules and unities), it was because thought is in the first instance so dominant and triumphant that it makes us forget language. "I wish he were dead . . . I don't dislike you . . . Voluptuous languor . . . War is war . . ." Whether it is literary or banal, a commonplace expression is an *event* of language which, from its very first appearance, delights our minds. It seems to lend itself to countless different meanings, which get progressively more profound, so incommensurable is its spiritual dimension with the part of it that is made up of words and matter. It appears to escape for a moment from the servitude of language, and we escape along with it. Which explains

---

2. We could give countless examples of this if it seemed useful. Among them, the following: Critics unanimously accused Roger Martin du Gard of giving his *Thibault* an ending—the death of Jacques Thibault—that was far too "novelistic" and, according to them, implausible. In fact, it is not in the least bit implausible; we have in real life seen more than one aviator die—Lauro de Bosis was one of them—because they were throwing pacifist tracts out of their aeroplane. But the illusion is easy to explain: It is not Jacques' death that is too novelistic. It is the novel that is not novelistic enough: Just before this death it is packed with texts, historical documents, scenes taken from real life, tracts and newspaper articles. The novelist is absent from all of this. So as a result, the merest attempt on his part to redirect events gives the immediate impression of being "novelistic," and false. Run away from the novel and it will catch up with you.

3. [Paulhan's source for this saying of the Stoics was quite possibly Jacques Casanova de Seingalt's (1725–1798) *Memoirs,* in the chapter entitled "Return to Paris," in which he writes: "There is no such thing as destiny. We ourselves shape our lives, notwithstanding that saying of the Stoics: Volentem ducit, nolentem trahit." *Trans.*]

no doubt why it makes such a strong impression on our memory, being the sign of a triumph.

All that we have discovered, then, is that a cliché needs—if it is to avoid becoming a sign of defeat and cowardliness—to be constantly rethought, put into question, cleansed. As if we needed to respond to this excess of meaning with an excess of language: to this excess of spirit with an excess of matter.[4] We might indeed name the Terrorists' error *angelism,* insofar as expression is for them reduced to thought. But Rhetoric demonstrates that it is concerned instead with maintaining balance and stability. The treatise *Paysages* invites the poet "to sit down with his legs crossed and, before writing, to spend a long time nurturing feelings of delicacy and distance in his heart."[5] And in his soul, a feeling of *compensation;* because every idea *costs* the same in words, every thought the same in language, if our patience in attending to the material is to have its reward in the spiritual.

❦ ❦ ❦   What an intolerable constraint for a married couple to find themselves committed to one another for a whole lifetime. Yet what these two lovers asked for, with force and of their own free will, was precisely to be committed to one another for a whole lifetime. The same is true of rhetoric: It may at first give the impression of being an intolerable and cold restraint. But it is up to us to rediscover within it, at every moment, the original joy of that first commitment, when our spirit accepted having a body, and delighted in it, and recognized that out of this risk, at every moment, comes our entire sense of nobility, and the dignity itself of this discovery or of its exchange.

We now see, at the entrance to the public park in Tarbes, this new sign:

> IT IS FORBIDDEN TO ENTER THE PARK
> WITHOUT CARRYING FLOWERS

---

4. And neither is a man who has never done any physical exercise more liberated from his body (even if he thinks of himself as having a pure soul) than one who exercises regularly and is in full control of his actions. The former is, on the contrary, narrowly constrained by his body: He is mechanical, and almost stereotyped.

5. Line 1200.

When all is said and done it was an ingenious measure, because the visitors, already overburdened with their own flowers, were hardly likely to think of picking any others.

A little while later, however, what happened was . . .

❦ ❦ ❦   *Everyone knows what happened. We can no doubt allow ourselves at this point to stop Terror's "View," or better still, its "Perspective," which is by and large appropriate to our time, and responds to our ongoing concerns. We cannot, however, simply talk about Rhetoric as if we had just invented it. It has been around for a long time. It has even been around for too long. And we know that it made itself so despised, not so long ago, that the only course of action left for an honest writer was to let it rot in its own chains.*

Anyone who pursues their investigation in this direction, who is suffocating because of Maintenance, and who patiently identifies the causes of his asphyxia, the reasons behind these causes and the perspectives implied by these reasons—in short, who applies the method we have tried to formulate here to the workings of rhetoric—finds that he is led to make a number of unexpected discoveries, such that he has to profoundly alter and, in a sense, reverse this method (without taking away any of its rigor), and even reverse his reflection itself. He must finally recognize in this metamorphosis and this reversal the precise figure of the mystery announced in rather vague terms to him by popular opinion, myths, and poets. This is what we will see in the work that follows on from this one.

No, these were not the problems I had in mind when I first undertook this study. But what happened subsequently was that I was surprised by them for want of taking them by surprise, and (if I may say so) they dealt with me because I failed to deal with them. There are thus glimmers of light, visible to whomever sees them, hidden from whomever looks at them; gestures which cannot be performed without a certain negligence (like some stars, or stretching your arm out to its full length). In fact, let's just say I have said nothing.

THE END OF
TERROR IN LITERATURE

Names Mentioned

Aicard, Jean (1848–1921): Popular French poet, novelist, and dramatist, whose works were deeply inspired by his native Provence. His most famous novel, *Maurin des Maures* (1908), is often favorably compared to Alphonse Daudet's *Tartarin de Tarascon*.

Albalat, Antoine (1865–1935): French writer and critic who was the author of a number of highly regarded works on French literature and the "art of writing." One of the texts Paulhan refers to, *Les Ennemis de l'art d'écrire* (1905), is a polemical engagement with his predecessors (such as Brunetière, Faguet, Gourmont, Lanson, and Fénelon), many of whom Paulhan mentions.

Apollinaire, Guillaume (1880–1918): French poet who was one of the leading figures in the technical innovation and experimentation that was taking place in the early twentieth century. He developed a quirky, casual, lyrical style which is exemplified in his most famous collections, *Alcools* (1913) and *Calligrammes* (1918). He was a close friend of avant-garde artists such as Picasso and Braque.

Aragon, Louis (1897–1982): Poet, novelist and essayist, and a founder, with Eluard and Breton, of French Surrealism. He was also a political activist and Communist spokesperson. His influence on the development of the novel, and on poetic theory, has been considerable.

Ariste: Character in Racine's *Phèdre*.

Arland, Marcel (1899–1986): French novelist who was, along with Gide and Mauriac, one of the great psychological novelists of the interwar period. He was a close friend of Paulhan's, and served with him on the editorial committee of the *Nouvelle Revue Française*. He published a largely biographical study of Paulhan in 1961, *La Vocation transparente de Jean Paulhan*.

Audiat, Pierre (Pierre Fontrailles) (1891–1961): French literary historian who collaborated with J. René Chevaillier on a number of popular and often reprinted anthologies of contemporary literature for schoolchildren.

Bajazet: Eponymous character in *Bajazet*, tragedy by Racine.

Bally, Charles (1865–1947): Swiss linguist who, together with Séchehaye, edited and published Ferdinand de Saussure's *Cours de linguistique générale* in 1916. Bally had been one of Saussure's students. He also published a *Traité de stylistique française* (1909), and in a series of essays that appeared as *Linguistique générale et linguistique française,* elaborated his own linguistics of the spoken word.

Balzac, Jean Louis Guez de (1594–1654): French author, whose published collections of letters earned him a considerable reputation. He was famous for the stylistic precision of his language, which although rather affected in manner, was influential in reforming French prose.

Barrès, Maurice (1862–1923): French novelist and nationalist politician. In his trilogy of novels, *Le culte du moi* (1888–91), he proclaimed the superiority of the individual over society. His nationalism later manifested itself as a profound hatred of Germany.

Belmont, Georges (Georges Pelorson) (1909–89): Poet, editor, anglicist, translator of Beckett, Joyce, Henry James, Henry Miller, and Anthony Burgess, and an important figure in the literary and publishing world after the war. He was one of the founders, along with Camille Schuwer, of *transition* (see entry under Eugène Jolas).

Benda, Julien (1867–1956): French novelist and critic. A humanist and rationalist, he was fiercely critical of the romantic philosophies and ideologies of his time, particularly that of Henri Bergson. He best known work is *La Trahison des clercs* [*The Treason of the Intellectuals*] (1927), in which he accused many of his contemporaries of abandoning truth in favor of political passions.

Bergson, Henri (1859–1941): French philosopher, awarded the Nobel Prize for Literature in 1927. Bergson argued that intuition is deeper than the intellect. Some of the major concepts for which he is known are "duration" (that is, real time is experienced as continuous duration, and not through separate operations of the instinct and the intellect), and the *élan vital* (creative impulse, or living energy). His early work attempted to integrate the biological sciences with a theory of consciousness. He was a leading intellectual, even cult figure, of his generation.

Bloch, Jean-Richard (1884–1947): French writer and journalist, who founded the review *L'Effort,* then along with Romain Rolland in 1922, co-founded *Europe,* a free-ranging review which celebrated European cultural diversity. A committed Communist, he also founded *Le Soir* with Louis Aragon in 1937, and was one of the leaders of the anti-fascist movement.

Bloy, Léon (1846–1917): French Catholic writer and social reformer who was violently opposed to religious conformism. His works, including autobiographical novels and a tribute to the Jews, *Salut par les Juifs* (1892), denounce social injustice and cruelty.

Boileau, Nicolas (1636–1711): French writer, a close friend of Molière and Racine, and the historiographer of Louis XIV, he was largely responsible for theorizing the ideals and aesthetics of literary classicism, particularly in his *Art poétique* (1674). He took the side of the Ancients in the "Quarrel of the Ancients and Moderns."

Bonald, Louis Gabriel Ambroise, Vicomte de (1754–1840): Counter-revolutionary French political and philosophical writer who believed firmly in political absolutism and ecclesiastical despotism.

Bordeaux, Henry (1870–1963): A practicing lawyer, Henry Bordeaux turned to writing in 1900, and went on to become one of the best-known regional novelists of his generation. His novels were mostly set in his native Savoie, and were a lyrical celebration of the traditional religious and moral values of the family.

de Bosis, Lauro (1901–31): Italian anti-fascist activist who famously flew over Rome on 3 October 1931 and distributed 400,000 anti-fascist tracts. The plane never returned, but soon after this *The New York Times* received and published a long letter, "The Story of My Death," which de Bosis had sent prior to his flight. His exploits make him the likely model for the hero of Roger Martin du Gard's final novel of the *Thibault* series.

Bost, Pierre (1901–1975): French writer and philosopher who was a student of the radical political philosopher Alain, to whom he later devoted a study, *Alain professeur* (1928). A large part of his correspondence with Paulhan concerns Alain's ideas. Bost was part of the literary Resistance during the Occupation.

Bourget, Paul (1852–1935): French novelist, critic, travel writer, and social commentator. His early novels were naturalistic, but he soon developed a more moralistic and analytical style, underpinned by his orthodox Catholic beliefs. His psychological studies of literature, such as his *Essais de psychologie contemporaine* (1883), made him one of the most respected critics of his time.

Brunetière, Ferdinand (1849–1906): Director of the prominent literary journal *Revue des Deux Mondes,* and Catholic writer, he went on to become one of the staunchest defenders of classical literature. His theory of the "evolution of genres" was intended to confirm the superiority of classicism over movements such as Naturalism, Romanticism, and Symbolism.

Carco, Francis (1886–1958): French poet and novelist, his writings often had as their subject the Bohemian life in Paris which he himself led.

Cecchi, Emilio (1884–1966): Italian critic and essayist, he was one of the editors of *La Ronda*. He published on English and American literature, and the history of art.

Chamfort, Nicolas de (1741–94): French moralist whose writings were very lucid and tragic in tone. He was one of the first writers to take up the Republican cause.

Chapelain, Jean (1595–1674): French man of letters and poet, and a close advisor to Richelieu and Colbert, Chapelain was one of the founders of *L'Académie Française* in 1634. He is credited with establishing the theory of dramatic unities as standard practice in classical theatre.

Chênedollé, Charles Lioult de (1769–1833): Romantic French poet who emigrated to Germany in 1791, where he visited Mme de Staël and Klopstock. On his return to France, he befriended Chateaubriand, and fell in love with his sister. His best-known work is *Le Génie de l'homme* (1807).

Claudel, Paul (1868–1955): French poet, playwright, and essayist who was a major figure on the literary landscape in the first half of the twentieth century, and who also had a long career as a diplomat. His works were inspired by his profound Catholic faith.

Comte, Auguste (1798–1857): French philosopher and social reformer, who pioneered the development of sociology as an empirical science, and of the classification of the sciences. He was one of the founders and major theorists of positivism.

Cros, Charles (1842–1888): French inventor and poet, who founded the *Revue du monde nouveau*. He was close to poets and artists such as Mallarmé and Manet. He died in obscurity, but his poetry was subsequently acclaimed by the Surrealists.

Curtius, Ernst Robert (1886–1956): Distinguished German literary critic whose studies of French writers such as Barrès, Balzac, and Proust stressed their importance to European culture as a whole. His focus was always on the large, overarching themes of European literature.

Decourcelle, Pierre (1856–1926): Popular French playwright and mystery novel writer, whose serialized *Mystères de New York* (1922) was also adapted for the cinema.

Delille, Abbé Jacques (1738–1813): Professor of Latin poetry at the Collège Royal. He translated Pope, Milton, and Virgil into French. His own poetry celebrated an idealized nature. He was imprisoned for a short time during the Terror, and was hostile to Revolutionary ideals.

Doriot, Jacques (1898–1945): A committed communist in his early years, Doriot began to espouse fascism during the 1930s. He formed the Parti Populaire Français after he was expelled from the Communist Party in 1934. He advocated collaboration with Germany even before the Second World War, and died in Germany in 1945.

Drieu la Rochelle, Pierre (1893–1945): French novelist, dramatist, and essayist. His first novels drew on his painful experiences during the First World War. He was involved for a while with the Dadaists, and flirted early on with communism, but his political ideology gradually evolved during the 1930s towards fascism. With Doriot he argued for a particularly French fascism, but he openly collaborated with the Nazis during the Second World War. He took over the *Nouvelle Revue Française* from Jean Paulhan during the Occupation until 1943, and under him it was explicitly pro-Nazi in tone and content. He was arrested after the Liberation, and accused of collaboration, but committed suicide in 1945 before being tried.

Droz, Gustave (1832–1895): French painter and writer. He is perhaps best known as the author of *Monsieur, Madame et Bébé,* a novel that was very progressive in its ideas about equality in marriage, and the importance of women's happiness.

Du Bos, Charles (1882–1939): French writer and literary critic who went against the grain of the intellectual, analytical tradition of French criticism in reading literature for its spiritual, intuitive qualities. He was close to Mauriac and Gide.

Duhamel, Georges (1884–1966): French biologist and medical doctor by profession, his first poems were unanimist in inspiration. His experience of human suffering led him to argue the need for a more compassionate and tolerant humanism, as expressed in his later works. His masterpiece was *La Chronique des Pasquier,* the history of a family and its epoch (1933–1945).

Fabre, Jean Henri (1823–1915): French entomologist, well known for his studies of insect behavior.

Faguet, Emile (1847–1916): French literary critic and historian. His prolific studies stimulated interest in French intellectual history of the 17th, 18th, and 19th centuries. His major work is *Jean-Jacques Rousseau* (5 volumes, 1911–13).

Fargue, Léon-Paul (1876–1947): Modernist French poet, whose work celebrated the Paris of the first half of the 20th century.

Fénelon, François de Salignac de la Mothe (1651–1715): Prelate and writer, famous for his charm and originality, who was a favorite of Louis XIV. His major work was *Les Aventures de Télémaque* (1699), which combined political pedagogy with an evocation of Antiquity. Considered an important predecessor by the Enlightenment philosophers.

Feuillet, Octave (1821–90): Conventionally moralistic French novelist and playwright, whose works, such as *Roman d'un jeune homme pauvre* (1857), were very popular during the Second Empire.

Fontanes, Louis de (1757–1821): French poet and essayist who went into exile in London during the Revolution. A close friend of Chateaubriand. His own poetry could be described as conventionally elegant.

France, Anatole (1844–1924): Generally acknowledged as one of the greatest French prose stylists of the end of the 19th and early 20th centuries, Anatole France had a profound influence on a whole generation of writers. He was the model for Bergotte in Proust's *A la Recherche du temps perdu*. He sided with Zola during the Dreyfuss affair, and was increasingly militant in his socialism, becoming one of the founders of *L'Humanité*.

Gautier, Théophile (1811–72): French Romantic poet whose later works, in particular *Emaux et camées* (1852), exemplified his fascination with the formal perfection and beauty of language. This emphasis on the importance of form in art inspired the poets who came to be known as the *Parnassiens*.

Goncourt, Edmond (1822–1896) and Jules (1830–1870): "Les deux Goncourt," as they were known, collaborated on a number of works of art history, art criticism, and Naturalist novels. Their *Journal,* which for forty years gave an intimate insight into Parisian society, was immensely popular at the time. The Goncourt Academy, and the prestigious annual prize it awards for French fiction, were established as a result of a bequest in Edmond's will.

Gourmont, Rémy de (1858–1915): French poet, novelist, dramatist, and leading critic of the Symbolist movement. He was firmly opposed to all that was traditional, and supported originality and novelty. He is well known for his linguistic studies, such as *Le problème du style,* to which Paulhan makes reference.

Graffigny, Madame de (1695–1758): French writer who was best known for her *Lettres d'une Péruvienne* (1747), and a play about the conditions for women at the time, *Cénie* (1750).

Gribouille: Stock character in French literature who became a synonym for a simpleton, and who was popularized by the Countess of Ségur (1797–1874). Paulhan is making reference to her story, "La soeur de Gribouille," in which Gribouille, the naïve boy, jumps into a stream to avoid getting soaked by the rain.

Guenne, Jacques (1896–1945): Swiss writer and well-known art historian who was married to Hélène Cingria, the niece of the writer Charles-Albert Cingria.

Guizot, François (1787–1874): French historian and politician. He had a brilliant early academic career as Professor of Modern History at the Sorbonne. His bourgeois liberalist views of the Revolution and subsequent events informed his antirepublicanism, and his support for a parliamentary monarchy.

Han Yu (768–828): One of the Tang dynasty's most influential poets and essayists, best known for his "ancient prose style."

Hölderlin, Friedrich (1770–1843): German poet who, after a career as a tutor, fell into madness and spent the last thirty-seven years of his life in an asylum. He is generally considered one of the greatest lyric poets of all time.

Hughes, Richard (1900–74): English novelist and playwright, best known for his first novel, quoted by Paulhan, *A High Wind in Jamaica* (1929), which is a tale about a group of children captured by pirates.

Huysmans, Joris Karl (1848–1907): French novelist and art critic who was initially one of the leading writers of the Naturalist school. Dissatisfied with the constraints of naturalist methods, he went on to become the key figure of *fin-de-siècle* decadent aesthetics. His best known text, *A Rebours (Against Nature)* (1884), is from this period.

Jacob, Max (1876–1944): Surrealist poet and painter whose work was both humorous and profoundly mystical. His critical study *Art poétique* (1922) was very influential. He died in a Nazi concentration camp.

Jaloux, Edmond (1878–1949): French writer and critic who was very receptive to the literature of other cultures, especially German. He also published essays and several novels.

Jammes, Francis (1868–1938): Provincial writer who reacted against Symbolism, and whose poetry was inspired by nature and the everyday, as well as by his Franciscan religion.

Jolas, Eugène (1894–1952): Editor of the avant-garde journal *transition* along with his wife Maria, Jolas described himself as an "American in exile in the hybrid world of the Franco-German frontier." His trilingualism, and his fascination with literary and linguistic innovation and experimentation, drew him naturally to James Joyce, whose early work he published in *transition,* and with whom he developed a close friendship. He also befriended many of the leading French writers of his time.

Joubert, Joseph (1754–1824): French moralist, whose reflections and moralistic maxims were published after his death by Chateaubriand, of whom he had been a close friend and advisor.

Jouffroy, Théodore (1796–1842): French philosopher who taught at the Ecole Normale Supérieure, the Collège de France and the Sorbonne. He was a member of the "Eclectic School," which took an extreme spiritualist view on the relationship between human psychology and physiology.

Jouhandeau, Marcel (1888–1979): Prolific French writer who was one of the most outspoken of collaborators during the Occupation, and a close lifelong friend of Jean Paulhan, despite their radically different political views. His work, autobiographical in origin, was a tortured and often cruel interrogation of men and of God.

Kelvin, Lord (Sir William Thomson) (1824–1907): British physicist who worked with many of the important French scientists of the 19th century, such as Carnot and Joule, and whose work in thermodynamics and electromagnetics was ground-breaking. Absolute zero temperature (or "degree Kelvin") is named after him.

La Bruyère, Jean de (1645–96): La Bruyère occupies an important place in the grand French tradition of moralists, alongside Montaigne and La Rochefoucauld. He is often seen as a precursor of the Enlightenment and the French Revolution because of his strong compassion for ordinary people.

Laforgue, Jules (1860–1888): French poet who was inspired by popular song, and whose supple, eloquent language expressed a kind of lyricism of everyday life.

La Harpe, Jean-François (1739–1803): French dramatist and critic. Author of several dramas and historical tragedies, his best known play is probably *Lycée, ou Cours de littérature ancienne et moderne* (1794).

Lamartine, Alphonse de (1790–1869): French Romantic poet of minor aristocratic birth who is best known for his perpetually anthologized poem "Le lac" ("The Lake"). He also had a significant political career first as a diplomat, then as a member of parliament.

La Rocque, Colonel de (1885–1946): Military officer who in 1931 became president of the Croix-de-Feu, a conservative, Catholic, French nationalist group. He was involved in right wing politics in the 1930s, but was far more moderate than extremists such as Maurras and Doriot.

Lasserre, Pierre (1867–1930): Prolific French historian of ideas, literary critic, and musicologist. Strongly influenced by Nietzsche and Wagner, he was drawn to the ideas of Charles Maurras and "L'Action Française," but he progressively distanced himself from its ideology.

Lautréamont, comte de (Isidore Ducasse) (1846–70): French writer who died young, and whose writings were unappreciated during his lifetime. His most famous work, *Les Chants de Maldoror,* was later exalted by the Surrealists for its intensity and stylistic originality, and they saw it as prefiguring the literary revolutions of the early twentieth century.

Léautaud, Paul (1872–1956): Somewhat eccentric French essayist, novelist, and writer of memoirs, whose most important works were his two diaries—*Jour-*

nal littéraire and *Journal particulier*—published in several volumes covering most of his life.

Lebon, Joseph (1765–95): Fanatical supporter of Robespierre during the period of the Terror, he was made mayor of Arras in 1793. He set up the Revolutionary Tribunal in Arras in 1794, and proceeded to carry out a policy of mass arrests and summary executions. He was guillotined shortly after Robespierre in 1795.

Lemaître, Jules (1853–1914): French dramatist and poet, also one of the most renowned literary and theatre critics of the end of the 19th and early 20th centuries in France. He was one of the chief exponents of "impressionistic" criticism.

Lièvre, Pierre (1882–1939): French literary critic and friend of Jean Paulhan, he produced an edition of Corneille's plays, and published widely in various literary reviews.

Loti, Pierre (1850–1923): A sailor by trade, Loti's novels were largely based on his experiences of other cultures on his travels. His representations of these cultures were highly exoticized, and nostalgic in tone.

Malot, Hector (1830–1907): French writer, author of many melodramatic novels although best known for his children's fiction, which present a realistic insight into French society at the end of the 19th century.

Marcel, Gabriel (1889–1973): French philosopher and dramatist who described himself as a "Christian existentialist." He rejected the abstract objectivity of contemporary science, and argued that only a subjectivity based on Christian incarnation could lead to a true understanding of Being.

Marchangy, Louis-Antoine-François de (1782–1826): French magistrate and minister, and author of a fairly conventional literary history of France entitled *La Gaule poétique.*

Marinetti, Filippo Tomasso (1876–1944): Italian writer who divided his time between the French and Italian literary scenes. He was the founder of, and chief publicist for, the Futurist movement. The work Paulhan refers to, *Words-in-Freedom,* is typical of the radical break with conventional poetic form and typography that Marinetti sought to introduce.

Marivaux, Pierre Carlet de Chamblain de (1688–1763): Most influential French playwright of the eighteenth century, who wrote many comedies for La Comédie française and La Comédie littéraire of Paris. The French word *marivaudages* was coined from the flirtatious, bantering style of his dialogue.

Martin du Gard, Roger (1881–1958): French writer whose major work was his epic series of novels tracing the history of a family, *Les Thibault,* from the

First World War to the outbreak of the Second. The novel Paulhan refers to is *L'Epilogue,* the final one in the series.

Maupassant, Guy de (1850–1893): French author who was generally acclaimed as the master of the short story form. His tales, naturalist in style, often had as their subject simple stories of ordinary people.

Maurois, André (Emile Herzog) (1885–1967): French writer, generally considered one of the great literary and historical biographers. His subjects included Byron, George Washington, Chateaubriand, Victor Hugo, Disraeli, and Proust.

Maurras, Charles (1868–1952): French writer and politician who was one of the founders of "L'Action Française." His virulent fascism and antisemitism made him a focal point for right wing intellectuals in the 1930s, and one of the most prominent collaborators during the Occupation.

Maury, Jean Siffrein (1746–1817): Churchman, and defender of the nobility and clergy before the Revolution, he was made archbishop of Paris in 1810. He was also a writer and literary historian known for his wit. Maury's guillotine dream was famously alluded to in chapter 6 of Freud's *Interpretation of Dreams,* where Freud discusses it as an example of a "secondary elaboration" of an unconscious fantasy.

Meillet, Antoine (1866–1936): French linguist who was a specialist of Indo-European languages and comparative grammar. He was influenced by the sociological theories of Emile Durkheim, and was interested in the social dimension of linguistics. His work is often referred to by Paulhan, if only as a foil for his own ideas about language.

Morand, Paul (1888–1976): French poet and novelist. A career diplomat, his knowledge of other cultures made him a truly cosmopolitan writer. His work offers an outstanding chronicle of Europe in the 1920s.

Moréas, Jean (Iannis Papadiamantopoulos) (1856–1910): Greek-born French writer who was drawn to the Decadent writers, and then to Symbolism, before advocating a return to a more neo-classical style. He founded *L'Ecole romane* with this objective in mind.

Natchez, les: Title of a long, rambling, sentimental prose epic by Chateaubriand written in 1800, inspired by his visit to Louisiana. It is an exoticized account of the massacre of the native American Natchez tribe by the French in 1727.

Nisard, Désiré (1806–88): French journalist, professor, and literary historian, he held a number of eminent positions in the civil service and education, including a spell as director of the Ecole Normale Supérieure (1857–62).

Noailles, Anna de (1876–1933): French poet, born into a noble Romanian family. She was famous for the literary gatherings at her home in Paris at the beginning of the 20th century. Her own poetry was personal and extremely lyrical, and she also wrote several novels and an autobiography.

Nodier, Charles (1780–1844): French novelist and poet whose literary salon, frequented by writers such as Hugo, Sainte-Beuve and Dumas père, was an important focal point for the Romantic movement. He was also a lexicographer, and his *Dictionnaire des onomatopées françaises* mentioned by Paulhan is from 1808.

Novalis, Friedrich von Hardenberg (1772–1801): German poet and thinker, widely considered to be the founder of Romanticism. His best known text is *Hymns to the Night* (1797)

Nyrop, Kristoffer (1858–1931): Danish linguist who was an expert on the French language. He published a *Grammaire historique de la langue française* (1899–1930), which is most likely the text Paulhan is alluding to.

Parain, Brice (1897–1971): Philosopher of language who was a long-time contributor to the *NRF*. Among his works are *Recherches sur la nature et la fonction du langage* (1942). He appeared, playing himself, in Jean-Luc Godard's film *Vivre la vie* (1962).

Paul, Hermann (1846–1921): German linguist, a specialist of comparative grammar.

Paulhan, Jean (1884–1968): Born in Nîmes, Paulhan studied literature and philosophy at the Sorbonne. He taught at a French lycée in Madagascar from 1908 to 1910, and then briefly taught Malagasy at the Ecole des Langues Orientales. He started work on a thesis on the "Semantics of Malagasy Proverbs," directed by Lucien Lévy-Bruhl. He served in the French army, and was wounded in action in 1914. His first publications were semi-autobiographical *récits,* and he became closely involved with Surrealist writers after the war. He became secretary of the *Nouvelle Revue Française* in 1920, and succeeded Jacques Rivière as editor in 1925. He had an increasingly influential role at the heart of the Parisian literary world. He left the *NRF* in 1941 when it was taken over by Drieu la Rochelle (see entry under this name). He was director of the relaunched *NNRF* between 1953 and 1963. He wrote on subjects as diverse as language and literature, modern painting, politics, poetic theory, Eastern mysticism, libertinage, etymology, and card games. His best known-work is *Les fleurs de Tarbes, ou la Terreur dans les lettres* (*The Flowers of Tarbes or, Terror in Literature*).

Péguy, Charles (1873–1914): French poet and writer who was initially a militant socialist, and the most passionate of defenders of Dreyfuss. He broke with the Socialist Party, and although he continued to work untiringly for humanitarian causes, his writing was increasingly marked by a profound spiritualism and mysticism. He is acknowledged as one of the foremost French Catholic writers.

Pelorson, Georges (1909–89): See entry under Belmont, Georges.

Petit Journal, le: Journal bought by La Rocque (see entry under his name) in 1937, and of which he became the director.

Planche, Jean Baptiste Gustave (1808–1857): Important French literary and art critic who was a fervent early admirer of George Sand and Alfred de Vigny, but his conservatism and classical aesthetic sensibility led him to be scornful of Romantic poets such as Hugo and Lamartine.

Plautus, Titus Maccius (254 B.C.–184 B.C.): The reference here is to the Latin comic poet, whose *Amphitryon* was redone by Molière, as it was by many other French dramatists.

Plessis, Frédéric (1851–1942): French poet and novelist, and a close friend of Anatole France, who had a decisive early influence on his choice of career as a University professor of literature. He taught at a number of universities before occupying the Chair of Latin Poetry at the Sorbonne.

Plisnier, Charles (1896–1952): Francophone Belgian poet, novelist, and essayist, who started out as a committed Marxist. His later novels were marked by a disillusionment with militant communism, and an increasing focus on personal and spiritual conflicts within a bourgeois milieu.

Pourtalès, Guy de (1881–1941): Swiss novelist and essayist who became a naturalized French citizen. His novels portrayed the world of the Swiss bourgeoisie during the period 1900–1914, and he published several biographical studies of musicians.

Pradon: Obscure writer who, encouraged by Racine's enemies, wrote a play entitled *Phèdre* which was performed two days after the first performance of Racine's *Phèdre*. The success of Pradon's work caused Racine to renounce writing for a time.

Prévost, Jean (1901–44): French poet and literary critic who was very active in the Resistance (alias capitaine Goderville), and was killed by the Nazis in 1944.

Proudhon, Pierre Joseph (1809–65): French social theorist, journalist, and writer, whom Marx called "the boldest thinker of French Socialism." He was one of the pioneers of mutualism and syndicalism, and a strong advocate of mass education.

Ramuz, Charles Ferdinand (1878–1947): Francophone Swiss writer whose novels portray the rural life in his native canton of Vaud.

Reinach, Joseph (1856–1921): French politician, and close ally of Léon Gambetta. He strongly defended Dreyfuss, and later wrote a 7-volume *Histoire de l'affaire Dreyfuss* (1931).

Renan, Ernest (1823–92): French philosopher and historian who attempted to reconcile his early Christian faith with rationalism and scientific progress. He wrote a number of important volumes on the history and philosophy of religion. His ideas influenced a whole generation of writers, among them Anatole France, Paul Bourget, and Charles Maurras (see entries under these names).

Renard, Jules (1864–1910): French realist and provincial writer whose journals, because of their classical style, were highly regarded.

Richelieu, Armand Jean du Plessis, cardinal de (1585–1642): French prelate and statesman, chief minister of Louis XIII, and cardinal of the Roman Catholic church. His policies ensured the consolidation of the absolute power of the monarchy.

Romains, Jules (1885–1972): French writer who is known for his long novel cycle, *Les hommes de bonne volonté* [*Men of Goodwill*] (1932–46), but also as a satirical playwright, and as the chief exponent of "unanimism," a theory which posited the existence of a collective spirit or personality.

Rostand, Edmond (1868–1918): French poet and dramatist. His early plays were charming and fanciful, and he is best known for his immensely popular romantic drama, *Cyrano de Bergerac* (1897).

Rougemont, Denis de (1906–1985): Francophone Swiss writer and philosopher who published widely on existentialism, and wrote a famous study on passion, *L'Amour et l'Occident* [*Love in the Western World*] (1939).

Sainte-Beuve, Charles Augustin (1804–69): Considered the most formidable French literary historian and critic of the 19th century. He was first of all attracted to Romanticism, but he eventually went on to teach and publish on a vast range of writers and periods. His critical method of appreciating literature through the psychological and biographical study of the writer was later famously challenged by Proust in his *Contre Sainte-Beuve*.

Sarcey, Francisque (1827–99): French journalist and well-known drama critic, who was a regular contributor to *Le Temps* and *Figaro*. His tastes were fairly conventionally bourgeois.

Schwob, Marcel (1867–1905): French writer and literary critic whose fiction was marked by his taste for the fantastic, and who published a number of literary studies, historical accounts and biographies.

Sorel, Georges (1847–1922): French journalist and left-wing political theorist who was one of the main advocates of revolutionary syndicalism.

Souday, Paul (1869–1929): French literary critic who was influential in helping to establish major early 20th century writers such as Gide, Proust, and Valéry.

Spencer, Herbert (1820–1903): English philosopher and sociologist who adapted Darwinian evolutionary theories and applied them to a vast synthetic explanation of all social phenomena. He was an unashamed apologist of individualism and free enterprise.

Taine, Hippolyte Adolphe (1828–1893): French critic and historian, whose socio-historical method had a far-reaching impact on literary criticism, philosophy and the social sciences. His deterministic theories were at the origin of the naturalistic school. Along with Ernest Renan (see entry under this name), he was the most influential intellectual figure of his generation. His best known work is the six-volume *Les Origines de la France contemporaine.*

Théramène: Character in Racine's *Phèdre.* The "monster" Paulhan is referring to appears in Théramène's famous account of Hyppolite's death by a mythological sea-creature.

Thibaudet, Albert (1874–1936): French literary critic whose work was indebted to Bergson (see entry under this name), and who was an important figure in the French literary world between the two wars.

Verlaine, Paul (1844–96): French poet who became an important writer of the bohemian literary scene in Paris, and a key figure in the Symbolist movement. He left his wife for his young protégé, Arthur Rimbaud, and together they traveled across Belgium and England, but their stormy relationship came to a violent end, with Verlaine imprisoned for 18 months after trying to shoot Rimbaud. Verlaine's poetry is distinguished by its haunting, melancholic tone, and its simple, musical style. Paulhan alludes elliptically to a famous quotation by Verlaine, who expresses a desire to "take eloquence and wring it by its neck."

Villiers de l'Isle-Adam, Auguste, comte de (1838–89): One of the leading figures of the Symbolist movement. A ferocious critic of science and positivism, of the bourgeoisie and its materialism, his work was by turns fantastic, lyrical, subversive, ironic, religious, and supernatural. Rémy de Gourmont (see entry under this name) famously described him as an "exorcist of the real."

Weil, Simone (1909–43): French philosopher whose writings on the major political and cultural themes of the age (revolution, progress, violence, rootedness, the state and the individual) were all closely bound up with her left-wing political activism, and her experiences of working class life. Her political thinking took an increasingly mystical turn toward the end of her life.

❦ ❦ ❦   I have been unable to trace any sources for the following names, even though a number of seductive, but ultimately speculative, theories have been proposed to me: Alerte, Père Botzarro, Hiliase, Innocent Fèvre, Juvignet, and Thérèse Thirion. These are quite possibly either apocryphal, or deliberate distortions of other names by Paulhan. Given his propensity for playful invention, this is more than likely to be the case.

MICHAEL SYROTINSKI is a professor of French at the University of Aberdeen, Scotland. He is the author of *Defying Gravity: Jean Paulhan's Interventions in Twentieth Century French Intellectual History* (1998) and *Singular Performances: Reinscribing the Subject in Francophone African Writing* (2002). He has previously co-translated a collection of Paulhan's *récits, Progress in Love on the Slow Side* (1994).

The University of Illinois Press
is a founding member of the
Association of American University Presses.

Composed in 10.5/13 Adobe Minion
with Bodoni Ornaments display
by Jim Proefrock
at the University of Illinois Press
Designed by Dennis Roberts
Manufactured by Maple-Vail
Book Manufacturing Group

University of Illinois Press
1325 South Oak Street
Champaign, IL 61820-6903
www.press.uillinois.edu